MINDING
THE BODY

WHAT STUDENT ATHLETES KNOW ABOUT LEARNING

JULIE CHEVILLE

Foreword by Bonnie Sunstein

Boynton/Cook
HEINEMANN
Portsmouth, NH

For my sister Carol

Boynton/Cook Publishers, Inc.
A subsidiary of Reed Elsevier Inc.
361 Hanover Street
Portsmouth, NH 03801–3912
www.boyntoncook.com

Offices and agents throughout the world

The author and publisher wish to thank those who have generously given permission to reprint borrowed material:

Cover photo of Tangela Smith, courtesy of Phillip Haddy, Sports Information Department, University of Iowa.

Library of Congress Cataloging-in-Publication Data
Cheville, Julie.
  Minding the body : what student athletes know about learning / Julie Cheville.
    p. cm.
  Includes bibliographical references and index.
  ISBN 0-86709-499-0 (alk. paper)
    1. College athletes—Education—United States.   2. Learning, Psychology of.
  I. Title.

  LC2580.6 .C44 2001
  378.1'9828'796—dc21   2001035780

Editor: Lisa Luedeke
Production service: Colophon
Production coordinator: Sonja S. Chapman
Cover design: Jenny Jensen Greenleaf
Manufacturing: Steve Bernier

Printed in the United States of America on acid-free paper
05 04 03 02 01 VP 1 2 3 4 5

Contents

Contents

Foreword

In ethnographic writing, a researcher has two sets of choices which often touch and sometimes collide: choices about which of the mass of notes, transcripts, printed material, and records to use (the "ethnoverbiage," I like to call it), and choices about how to render all of that data into a compelling piece of writing for a reader (the "shape" of the "story" that emerges). And in the process, researcher/writers ask agonizing questions about the job. What ideas are important for my reader to know? Whose voices are important to hear? Who speaks loudest? Are they still authentic voices even though I've filtered them through my notes and tapes? How do I best represent the several years worth of talking, listening, observing, reading, learning, and thinking that I've experienced with these topics, these people, these places? How do I guide my reader in a verbal journey similar to the experiential one I've taken? How do I make the roads seem smooth and the turns seem curved when my real ride was bumpy, long, foggy, and multi-directional? Or do I? And most important, how much shall I share of myself—my background, my interests, my opinions, my passions, with my reader? What do I admit about me? These are essential, ethical questions for researchers and writers in many disciplines, important questions no one wants to compromise—yet questions no writer/researcher ever feels complete about answering.

Julie Cheville has asked and answered such questions with courage and creativity. And through her elegant writing, we learn her answers without compromise. As we read *Minding the Body*, we take her journey as well as the journeys of the student athletes we are privileged to meet on her pages. She offers herself as a guide in multiple dimensions. Because of her careful reflexive stance as a writer, Julie is a first person teacher-guide who works tirelessly as a passionate and disciplined advocate for student athletes. Because of her impeccable and thorough scholarship, she takes us on a first person academic trip through some tangled and fascinating interrelationships between mind and body, the academy and sport, tutors and students, coaches and athletes, practice sessions and classroom practice, racial difference and racial equity as it shows itself in the assumptions of fans, journalists, policy makers, administrators, teachers, students, and families. Because of her analysis, Julie serves as our first-person tutor as she introduces us to new ideas and terms such as "conceptual diversity," "embodied cognition," "schematic portability," "redundant layers of academic support." She investigates the system of racial politics, social assumptions, national assessment practices, high-revenue intercollegiate sports behaviors, and shares her mediations about what she learns. Like a well-prepared tutor, she offers excerpts and interpretations of the disciplines, theories, opinion pieces, and histories we need in order to understand what's behind the story of these athletes as they come to know school and school comes to know them. She offers honest observations with phrases like "the fine line between academic support and fraud" and, whether we agree or not, we can accept her opinion because she's let us know all along who she is as our guide.

Finally, as a multidisciplinarian, she draws from many areas of scholarship—and explains their theories—in order to be thorough about what she sees, hears, and thinks along the way: the anthropology of performance, literacy studies, cultural studies, journalism and political science, biogenetic and medical research, sociological theories about group behavior.

Julie makes these connections in her research and writing so that her knowledge becomes our knowledge as we watch her observations come alive on the basketball court, in the training rooms, in the classroom, and quite literally on the chair in her office. The student athletes talk with us as they talk with Julie, explaining to her—and to us—how they know what they know and what they might need that they don't currently have in order to know more.

Knowledge, for them, for Julie, and now in this book for us, suddenly becomes a verb as active as an athlete moving on a playing field. Educational theorist Elliott Eisner recognizes that in any acccount of someone's research, knowledge and experience are inextricably linked:

> Knowledge is not an inert material discovered through research, it is a functioning aspect of human cognition, a resource that lives in the biographies, thoughts, and actions of individuals, not something that one can stockpile and point to. For knowledge to be, it must be known. To be known, someone must act upon it. In short, knowledge is a verb. (210)

In this lucid account of her research, Julie links her knowledge as the student-athletes teach her and, in turn, teach us. We meet Billy, Tangela, Malikah, Simone, Anthony, and Nadine, their teammates, coaches, and some of their teachers. We feel their pain and triumph, at play, at school, and at leisure. We eat with them and study with them. We listen to their complaints, hear their questions, share their humor, see their observations, and engage with them in their critiques and dilemmas. These student athletes, their stories, their dazzling differences as thinkers and learners offer the substance that holds together this book and makes sense of the complexities Julie invites us to think about.

And so this book, its author, its ideas, and its main characters, forges the links that enable us to learn as we're learning about others' learning. We enjoy a continuous interaction between intellectual content and individual experience, between mind and body, between doing and perception, between the people whose portraits Julie paints and the academic interpretations and intricate histories she builds. Educational philosopher John Dewey described these links in his classic *Education and Experience* in 1934: "As we manipulate, we touch and feel. As we look, we see; as we listen, we hear. The hand moves with etching needle or with brush. The eye attends and reports the consequence of what is done. Because of this intimate connection, subsequent doing is cumulative . . . the relation is so close that it controls simultaneously both the doing and the perception. (49)"

I have seen this book emerge from many years of study, talking, record keeping, interpreting, thinking, and acting. In short, in Dewey's words, I watched Julie move continuously and fluently between "the doing and the perception." With my own reflexive stance, I can tell you that her project answered many questions for me, made connections I'd not thought to think about, taught me about literacies I'd not considered, and expanded my definition of what one needs to know in order to know. I remind myself that it was the choices she and her student athletes made, about what to write and how to write it, that makes this a book I'd want to share with any interested person who has ever taken a course, taught a course, or attended an intercollegiate game. I expect it will do the same for you.

Bonnie S. Sunstein
Associate Professor, English and Education
University of Iowa

Works Cited

Bateson, M. C. 1994. *Peripheral Vision: Learning Along the Way.* New York: Harper Collins.

Dewey, J. 1934/1980. *Art as Experience.* Perigree/G.P. Putnam's.

Eisner, E. 1990. *The Enlightened Eye: Qualitative Inquiry and the Enhancement of Educational Practice.* New York: Macmillan.

Acknowledgments

I am most grateful to Tangela Smith. Words do not capture her influence. I also thank Karen Clayton Lange, Nadine Domond, Simone Edwards, Stacy Frese, Tiffany Gooden, Angie Hamblin, Amy Herrig, Susan Koering, Jenny Noll, Shannon Perry, and Malikah Willis, students and athletes who deepened my understanding of what it means to learn and know.

I recognize the assistance of head trainer Roxann Dahl, chef Jim Esch, and managers Nealie Hiersch, Rani Peyton, Jeremy Venenga, and Michael Widen. Sherilyn Fiveash, Paula Jantz, and Taunya Tinsley were members of the University of Iowa women's athletic administration at the time of this study and offered support. For their trust and accessibility, I am indebted to coaches Angie Lee, Bonnie Henrickson, Linda Myers, and Rose Peeples. In particular, I am grateful to Linda Myers for invaluable assistance late in production. I also appreciate the help of Phillip Haddy, director of sports information at the University of Iowa.

I thank staff and students associated with the Office of Athletic Student Services from 1986–1995. I am indebted to Greg Isaac and to the many students who led me to rethink my instructional theory and practice.

During my doctoral work in the Language, Literacy, and Culture program at the University of Iowa, I learned from Ralph Cintron, Carolyn Colvin, Anne DiPardo, James Marshall, and Mary Trachsel. Cheryll Harcourt, my peer in the graduate program, assisted me to envision a performance-sensitive project. I also acknowledge Elizabeth Chiseri-Strater and Susan Birrell.

As a visiting professor of English at Drake University, I benefited from contact with Bruce Horner, Joseph Lenz, Min-Zhan Lu, Elizabeth Robertson, Jody Swilky, and Thomas Swiss. A year later, as an adjunct faculty member in the department of English at Ohio State University, I received support from LaVerne Browand, Cheryl Frasch, Lucinda Kirk, Beverly Moss, Margi Sheehy, and Mindy Wright. At Elizabethtown College, I acknowledge Terry Blue, Angela Kohlweiler, Becky Olson, and Carmine Sarracino. I thank Lesley Morrow, Michael Smith, and Dorothy Strickland at Rutgers University.

At Boynton/Cook, I am grateful to editor Lisa Luedeke, who supported this unusual project throughout the course of its evolution. Her insights, in addition to critical yet encouraging response from several reviewers, assisted me to clarify my thinking and writing. For their expedient and careful work, I acknowledge production coordinator Sonja S. Chapman at Heinemann and Denise Botelho at Colophon.

I am indebted to dear friends. Margaret Finders, a thoughtful reader, provided formative response from the onset of fieldwork while Cynthia Lewis shared and supported my early interest in performance theory. Throughout the project, Carol Severino's care and insight proved vital. Bonnie Sunstein, an extraordinary mentor, secured grants and scholarships that allowed me the time and material security necessary to work well and learn deeply. Without her mind and spirit, this interdisciplinary project would not have progressed.

For their steadfast care, I thank my siblings John and Anne and my brother-in-law Chris. For their joy, I am grateful to Amy, Stephen, and Jan. My parents Norman and Beth have supported my learning with care and conviction. Finally, I acknowledge the lasting influence of my grandparents, rural Iowans who cultivated land and lives with love.

Introduction

. . . we have bodies connected to the natural world, such that our consciousness and rationality are tied to our bodily orientations and interactions in and with our environment. Our embodiment is essential to who we are, to what meaning is, and to our ability to draw rational inferences and to be creative.

Mark Johnson,
The Body in the Mind (1987)

When we met, Billy was a first generation college student whose football scholarship had enabled him to attend the University of Iowa. Identified as academically "at-risk," he was required by the Office of Athletic Student Services to receive tutorial support, the point at which our work together began. Billy came from a low-resource school district that lacked sufficient library and curricular materials. Still, he struck me as capable of acquiring the reading and writing strategies necessary to succeed. An African American athlete on a predominantly white campus, Billy feared his professors might not take him seriously as a student, perhaps even assume he was intellectually inferior to his peers. By virtue of his race and unmistakably athletic physique, Billy felt vulnerable.

Meeting on a weekly basis, I introduced Billy to strategies and academic conventions for reading and writing. During and after our study sessions, he shared anecdotes and memories that assisted me to understand his educational history. From the beginning, Billy characterized his life and learning in terms of a guiding metaphor. Articulated in a

1

host of variants, his "playing the game" was neither a rhetorical device
nor a sports cliché.

> To me, it [university schooling] seems like a whole big game. I gotta
> play . . . so that I can get out of here with a degree and with what I
> need to survive in this other bigger game of life. That's what I want to
> do. Become an important part in this game and make some things
> happen. It's like Martin Luther King said about the nonviolence
> movement. How you turn the other cheek? If you want to survive,
> or excel, in America, you gotta do some things. You gotta take some
> things.

As Mark Johnson (1987) and George Lakoff (1989) argue, the metaphors that take root in our consciousness arise from patterns of bodily
activity. Billy's descriptions of home and school often tapped into the
life-as-game metaphor. Oriented toward "survival," Billy believed that
academic success would insure his participation in social change. His
metaphorical understanding, articulated through language, suggested
that racial and material inequities had situated his thought in ways
that attuned him to performative dilemmas across experiential contexts. The irony was that while Billy's conceptual orientation attested
to the interrelationship of mental and bodily activity, he struggled to
understand himself as a thinker.

Illustrating what W. E. B. DuBois (1990) termed "double consciousness," Billy interpreted his life and learning through the lens of white-
ness. In his view, being and knowing were mutually exclusive conditions. Status as a laboring body resulted from disadvantages that
removed one from intellectual opportunities. According to Billy, one's
access to privilege influenced whether he was acculturated to be *or* to
think. As he explained,

> Maybe the reason why Black athletes seem to be better athletes is be-
> cause when we were younger, you all—white people—were taught
> to think with your minds, you know? Black people were taught to do
> things athletically. Another person told me this story. He said, when a
> white person goes to his father and says, "Daddy, I want an airplane."
> Okay, the father will go out and buy him a model airplane, and he [the
> white child] will go and just put it together, fix it, and do whatever.
> And the Black child will go to his father, and his father will give him
> an airplane with a string on it, so he can pull it. Right there, at a young
> age, we're conditioned to think two different ways. To work from the
> neck down, that's our work. But with the white kid, he's going to buy
> something, or he's going to make it to be for his own use and some-
> thing for himself. He's taught to work from the neck up, you know
> what I mean?

According to this anecdote, acculturation into either being *or* thinking
results from the realities of one's bodily place and history. In Billy's

mind, "the Black child" learns to work "from the neck down," set apart from those who possess the means and encouragement to labor intellectually. As I listened to Billy, I worried about the devaluation he attributed to his own body. Though I remembered bell hooks's (1993) claim that the conditions of urban life can often lead "Black folks . . . to accept a mind/body split" (180), I began to wonder to what extent Billy's activity within the university might be reinforcing his destructive perspective.

An Institutional Divide: Knowing vs. Being

In mid-size and large public universities, the separate function of athletic and academic domains reinforces a longstanding philosophical distinction between thought and action. For student athletes whose bodies are already a source of insecurity, the fragmented domains can be damaging. In the athletic sphere, those who participate in major revenue sports find their lives temporally and spatially restricted, required by athletic support personnel to enroll in the same courses, eat at the same training tables, study at the same learning centers, and reside in the same dormitories. According to a 1987 study sponsored by the Presidents Commission, a subcommittee of the National Collegiate Athletic Association (NCAA), 50 percent of those intercollegiate student athletes interviewed acknowledged a feeling that they lacked control of their academic lives. Removed from nonscholarship students and from opportunities to negotiate their schooling, respondents reported significant degrees of alienation. According to the study, African American student athletes acknowledged greater feelings of academic disempowerment than their white counterparts.[1]

In the university classroom, faculty who believe intellectual labor necessitates a mythic transcendence of mind over matter may fail to recognize, or even reject, the bodily dilemmas that situate students' conceptual orientations. Faculty who view the phrase "student-athlete" as paradoxical are guided by what bell hooks (1994) cites as the "romantic notion of the professor . . . as a mind that . . . is always at odds with the body" (137). A newspaper commentary written by Fern Kupfer (1995), a professor of English at Iowa State University, arises from this tradition,

> Every season in the newspaper there's the litany of offenses committed by student athletes: drug possession, forgery, domestic abuse, assault, theft, armed robbery. We continue to make bail. Make excuses. Set them free. A part of us feels betrayed that these kids are messing up the chance that they have to make something of themselves. Aren't we giving them a free education, for crying out loud? (9A)

Kupfer issues this sweeping indictment before advising, "Get rid of the hired thugs we call student athletes" (9A). Here, Kupfer enforces the divide between mind and body. Totalizing allusions to physical and property crime allow her to consolidate ideological power and privilege as an intellectual who must bear the burden of student athletes' criminality. While the Student Right-to-Know and Campus Security Act of 1990 mandates the disclosure of campus crime statistics, there exists no separate category for intercollegiate student athletes. However, given that hundreds of male and female students represent *each* of over a thousand NCAA Division I, II, and III member institutions, Kupfer's remark may be less an accurate characterization of this constituency than an indication of what student athletes most fear—that their athleticism will be appropriated and used against them by those who have the power to deny or devaluate their presence.

Certainly, faculty members have a legitimate right to scrutinize their athletic budgets, particularly in those institutions where general college funds are diverted to athletic coffers. In addition, both faculty and students have reason to question policies that grant student athletes inordinate residential or academic privileges. What critics like Kupfer must realize, however, is that blame targeted expressly at student athletes, though expedient, is rarely an effectual means of initiating institutional change. Peter McLaren (1995) warns that categorical claims that posit blame "relieve teachers from the need to engage in a form of pedagogical self-scrutiny or a serious critique of their personal roles within the school, and the school's role in the wider society" (211).

In the context of public and institutional debate about the role of intercollegiate student athletes it is not surprising that Billy understood his academic success as necessitating extreme levels of guardedness. He acknowledged that playing his various "games" successfully was contingent upon circumventing danger. Guided by an abstract orientation that attuned him to resistance or defense, Billy strove never to be caught "off guard."

> When I'm here [at the university] I'm on my guard, and when I go home, I'm on my different guard. Even when I'm at home, when I go out, I'm enjoying myself, but I never go out alone because you never know what could happen. I always go out with a friend. I'm always watching my back, you know? Basically, I play different games . . . trying to make sure nobody's gonna catch me off guard. Even when I'm walking up to my house [at home] from coming out late, I'm still watching [looks over both shoulders] and making sure, you know? Somebody might come running from the side of the house and want to take my car. Or somebody might have broken into my house. I always have those fears that somebody could be in there already and,

you know, do whatever and I'd have to defend myself. And, you know, would I be ready? I can honestly say that when I'm here [at the university] or I'm at home, there's a game that I'm playing.

To maintain his defensive orientation, Billy expended incredible emotional energy. Because concrete experiences at the university resonated, at least emotionally, with those at home, Billy had mapped his metaphorical understanding on to this domain. According to Mark Johnson (1987), figurative networks like Billy's "represent a pervasive mode of understanding by which we project patterns from one domain of experience in order to structure another domain of a different kind" (xiv–xv). In the same manner, Nancy Scheper-Hughes (1993) discovered that the concrete experience of drought for impoverished women and children of a northeastern Brazilian shantytown had abstract consequences, "capturing the imagination of people who are inclined to describe all that is bad in terms of dryness and who sometimes project the image of drought onto their own bodies" (69).

Difficulties accelerated the spring of Billy's sophomore year when university doctors detected cartilage damage that athletic personnel suspected might interrupt his performance on the field. Ultimately, Billy agreed to the preventive surgery from which he would never recover. Frustrated by a slow rehabilitation, Billy's hope waned. While he attached a stigma to his athleticism and believed others did as well, Billy had always appreciated that his athletic scholarship afforded him educational opportunities unavailable by any other means. Nonetheless, Billy entered his junior year feeling little connection to the academic realm. Because the Office of Athletic Student Services assumed responsibility for communication with Billy's professors, he hesitated contacting them himself. As long as professors sent written early warning and midterm reports to his academic advisor, Billy believed he could contribute little to the information already exchanged between athletic and academic personnel. As a result, he was often the last to understand his academic status. While I encouraged Billy to meet with instructors who seemed receptive, his anxiety about initiating appointments and conversations with faculty proved formidable.

The fall of his junior year, Billy's physical recovery was reversed by injury, and he found himself largely alone. No longer a contributing member to successes on the field, his relationships with teammates abated. While they practiced, he rehabilitated. While they recounted plays and games, he listened. While they participated, he watched. No longer deemed important even to the athletic enterprise, Billy found himself without purpose and without peers. As the fall semester progressed, Billy's spirit and academic progress nose-dived. His language, increasingly cynical, evidenced a dramatic shift in understanding.

> Being on the football team makes me feel like a house nigger. When I say "house nigger" I mean a person, a Black person, who really thinks more highly of either the white race or a white master than he thinks of himself. You know, like Malcolm X said of the plantation owner and the house nigger who lived in the house and ate the best food? The plantation owner would be sick and he [the house nigger] would say, "What's the matter, boss? *We* sick?" It's all about the person who has power.

With the mind–body split internalized in ways that had encouraged him to align feelings of self worth to physicality, Billy's identity had hinged upon escape from injury. With surgery and subsequent impairment, Billy's anecdotes suggested that his metaphorical understanding was undergoing semantic change. No longer cognizant of himself as a player in the various contexts he inhabited, Billy referred to his status as a "pawn" and "field Nigger," allusions that indicated his understanding of slavery and sport had coalesced. Billy's eventual references to the "house nigger" revealed the passive complicity he associated with immobility. Late in the fall of his junior year, Billy withdrew from the university.

Billy's embodied understanding had obligated him to guardedness, to the prospect of winning or losing, and to the strategic adjustment to context. Early in his university career, Billy aspired to be "important." By the time he withdrew, however, Billy felt little sense of agency. A destructive mind–body split internalized by the concrete forces of racial and material inequity before he came to the university had converged with an ideological divide embodied in the very structure of the institution he attended.

In effect, the autonomous function of academic and athletic domains did not challenge Billy's belief that he was merely a body sans intellect. Isolated within an athletic enterprise that privileged his athleticism, he had little occasion to understand his significance to the university as anything but physical. If one layers onto Billy's struggle broader public assumptions about the "hired thug" or "dumb jock," as well as animalizing images manufactured by sports journalists and commercial advertisers, the obstacles to academic empowerment prove formidable.

Embodied Cognition: Reconciling Mind and Body

In 1969, Arthur B. Jensen, a professor of educational psychology at the University of California-Berkeley, suggested that African American students are genetically predisposed to cognitive disadvantage and thereby inclined to learn by doing, or "associational learning" rather than by abstract thought. His deterministic claims remain abhorrent on two counts. First, such a view ascribes intellectual deficit to racial difference. As I describe in the Afterword, eugenic arguments attuned to bodily difference have long insured that cognitive status and educational opportunity belong to those who occupy privileged locations in a host of binaries (*white*/non-white, *male*/female, *able*/disabled). Second, such a view insists that pedagogies which encourage students to make concrete connections to content and to each other are inherently less conceptual than those that transmit information.

For several decades, qualitative researchers have challenged the traditional view that thought is solely an intramental experience. Documenting the relationship of context and cognition, researchers across the social sciences have identified how thought emerges from being and being-in-the-world. In a landmark study Sylvia Scribner and Michael Cole (1981) noted how varying contexts and uses of literacy among the Liberian Vai fostered distinct cognitive skills. Challenging the "great divide" forged between preliterate and literate thought, they revealed how cognitive skills of nonschooled individuals were different but no less logical than those of schooled writers. Their work introduced many to Lev Vygotsky, whose translations accelerated interest in how social mediation influences language and cognition. More recently, scholarship in "situated cognition" has considered how patterns of activity (Engestrom et al. 1999; Kirshner & Whitson 1997; Scribner 1990; Walkerdine 1997, 1998; Wertsch, Del Rio, & Alvarez 1995) and community (Lave 1997; Lave & Wenger 1991; Rogoff 1995; Wenger 1998) mediate thought.

Because the central focus of scholarship in the area of situated cognition has centered upon the mediating influence of symbol making, most notably language, the tradition has not squarely challenged a longstanding philosophical and scientific devaluation of the human body as an avenue to meaning. Given recent accounts of the link between cognition and bodily activity (Damasio 1994, 1999; Johnson 1987), there is reason to expand the notion of "situativity" to include the influence of the body upon the mind. In this way, studies of knowledge acquisition will begin to consider how thought is situated in both symbolic *and* bodily activity. Like James Whitson (1997), I do not see a theoretical disjuncture between studies of situated and embodied cognition. Whether the primary unit of analysis is social or bodily activity, researchers acknowledge the conceptual significance of human action. The important distinction is that while the concept of embodiment holds variable meaning across disciplines, embodied cognition acknowledges the interdependence of mind and body.[2]

How the human body is oriented in the context of activity determines what cognitive structures are available to learners. Documenting how thought is situated in bodily activity challenges a historical devaluation of the human body that has had several consequences. First, to the extent that language has been understood as liberating one from bodily "constraints," theories of cognition have accorded exclusive attention to symbolic influence. Second, for those understood in terms of bodily difference, the devaluation of the body has been the means by which individuals and cultural groups are made to bear the stigma of physicality, what is often a simultaneous indictment of intellect. Concern for how cognition is embodied upends the traditional rhetorical and philosophical insistence that language liberates one's mind from the material conditions of her body. In effect, embodied cognition reasserts how, for all students, denial of the body erases ways not just to be but to think.

The Stigma of Athleticism

During nearly a decade of work in the Office of Athlete Student Services, I grew aware of a fundamental tension that characterized the lives and learning of many with whom I worked. As athletes, these students relied on a partnership of mind and body for both individual and team performances. As they characterized their learning, I sensed that the conceptual orientation central to knowledge acquisition in sport was relatively useless in college classrooms that disassociated cognition from concrete activity and interaction. The conceptual disjunctures student athletes described seemed further complicated by an overarching ideological divide between academic (thought) and athletic (body) domains. Operating largely independent of each other, these institutional contexts seemed to preempt appreciation for cognition as situated in symbolic and bodily activity.

Two years after Billy's withdrawal, I grew interested in a qualitative study that might document the learning of intercollegiate student athletes at the University of Iowa, an NCAA Division I institution. Because nationwide graduation rates for participants in football and men's and women's basketball have traditionally inspired concern, I desired access to one of these team sports. The 1999 NCAA graduation rate report indicates that among those intercollegiate student athletes who entered college in 1993, received athletic aid, and maintained full-time academic status, only white football players suffered a reversal in matriculation, falling from 61 percent to 55 percent in the 1998 survey.[3] While nationwide graduation rates for African American student athletes in high-profile sports have risen and currently surpass those of African American students not on athletic scholarship, they still fall below figures registered for the general student body.

My experiences with administrative staff in both men's and women's athletic departments suggested the latter program might respond with greater openness and flexibility to a qualitative study. Because the women's athletic program was one of a select few in the country that did not fall under the jurisprudence of a men's administration, the staff possessed notable autonomy in hiring, facilities management, and marketing decisions. Unlike its male counterpart, the women's administration was less compartmentalized and hierarchical, a structure that would not demand recurring appeals for access at each turn in the study. At the same time I was interested in understanding how a streamlined administrative structure framed the learning of female student athletes, who were accorded considerable responsibility for their own academic welfare. Given my own experiences as a high school basketball player and coach, I also felt better positioned to assess the embodied cognition of female learners. Nevertheless, as I discuss in the Afterword, monitoring the influence of my embodied history as a white, middle-class woman would require a host of reflexive strategies throughout the stages of fieldwork and writing.

In the fall of 1995 I discussed the possibility of a formal study with Tangela, a member of the University of Iowa women's basketball team whom I had tutored for over a year. A conscientious yet apprehensive student, Tangela had sought my assistance voluntarily. My tutor log indicates we met regularly her freshman year, approximately 328 hours. Increasingly, our work brought me into contact with other members of the women's basketball team. Though obviously distinct in terms of gender and thereby removed from the particularly insidious cultural assumptions attached to African American masculinity, the female student athletes with whom I worked acknowledged that they, too, struggled with their athleticism.[4] Nadine, an off guard on the team, remarked,

> I'm a Black woman who plays sports. The Black community is only known for entertainment and sports and not known for being doctors, lawyers, or great minds. I have to fight against that day in and day out. I constantly fight against that, to try to prove that I do have a mind. God has blessed me with something, and I'm here to learn.

Nadine's "fight" was complicated by her location in an intercollegiate sports enterprise that made her visible to the public only by way of her physical accomplishments. Her athleticism posed little challenge to a predominantly white public that "has historically sought entertainment,

profit, and forms of racial reconciliation that do not challenge fundamental assumptions about racial difference" (Hoberman 1997, 4).

To exert power on the court does more than jeopardize a student
athlete's intellectual self-worth. As sociologist of sport David Whitson
(1994) suggests, girls and women often participate in sport understanding that "To succeed as an athlete can be to fail as a woman, because she has, in certain profound symbolic ways, become a man" (36).
Enacting bodily activity traditionally reserved for males, female student
athletes understand that their physicality on the court invites public
scrutiny not just of intellect but of sexual identity. Tangela noted,

> Some think most female athletes are gay. You just have to fight it. You
> have to show them that you're not. You've got to act all feminine . . .
> so you dress all fancy and stuff. And it may not be what you want to
> do. If a boy up here [at the university] tries to talk to you and you
> don't talk to them, they automatically think you're gay. But if you do
> talk to them, then everybody else calls you a whore.

For Tangela, public scrutiny of her physicality was influential. To com-
pensate for her power on the court, she reasserted her femininity by
dressing "all fancy and stuff." Through changes in comportment and
dress, Tangela felt she reassured the public of her sexual identity. Ironically, these performative adjustments contributed to the dilemmas
Tangela faced in the context of her relationship with male peers.

Prior to the start of the 1995–1996 season, with Tangela's encouragement, I introduced myself and the study to Angie Lee, first-year
head coach of the women's basketball program. Several days later, after
conferring separately with Tangela and me, Lee invited me to practice
so that I might introduce my project to team members (see Table 1),
who unanimously approved the study. On November 28, 1995, I began
attending daily practices and team breakfasts, and on December 1, to
avoid a conflict of interests, I resigned as a tutor in the men's athletic
department.

Upon my arrival in the field, I offered my tutoring services to all
members and managers of the women's basketball team. The effort was
a gesture of reciprocity in light of their collective agreement to participate. For the two-year duration of the study and the year of writing
that followed, I made myself available to team members during the day
and evening. In what became an inverted tutorial relationship, participants addressed my naivete, memory lapses, and questions. By the end
of the first season, I had observed the athletic learning of members of
the women's basketball team for a total of 307 hours, which included
73 practices and morning training tables and 17 home and away games.
During the second year of fieldwork, I analyzed participants' academic
learning.

Table 1.
Student Athletes and Coaches, 1995–1996

Players	Height	Class	Position	Hometown	Race
Karen	5-5	Sr.	Guard	Raleigh, NC	European American
Nadine	5-9	Soph.	Guard	Bridgeport, CT	African American
Simone	6-4	Sr.	Center	Kingston, Jamaica	African Caribbean
Stacy	5-8	Fr.	Guard	Cedar Rapids, IA	European American
Tiffany	6-0	Soph.	Forward	Fort Wayne, IN	African American
Angie	6-0	Soph.	Guard	Gary, IN	African American
Amy	6-4	Fr.	Center	Dubuque, IA	European American
Susan	5-9	Jr.	Guard	Stanwood, IA	European American
Jenny	6-5	Jr.	Center	Muscatine, IA	European American
Shannon	6-1	Sr.	Forward	Carson, CA	African American
Tangela	6-4	Soph.	Center	Chicago, IL	African American
Malikah	6-2	Soph.	Center	Cleveland, OH	African American

Coaches	Rank	Race
Angie Lee	Head coach	European American
Bonnie Henrickson	Assistant	European American
Linda Myers	Assistant	European American
Rose Peeples	Assistant	African American

Minding the Body

Work in situated cognition that has followed Scribner and Cole's Vai research illustrates how studies of knowledge acquisition in nontraditional settings can disclose relationships and activities that may well assist teachers to understand, even transform, knowledge-making in their classrooms. Extending the notion of activity, or practice, to include the spatial and temporal orientation of the human body, this study challenges the view that bodily activity reflects one of a host of "intelligences" (Gardner 1983). Such distinctions risk reducing learners to labels without disrupting the significant philosophical divide between mind and body that has long stymied accounts of what it means to learn and know. As a counterpoint, this book argues that for all learners, bodily activity gives rise to, and is subsequently mediated by, embodied mental structures. To the point, the body matters for all learners.

In Chapter One I examine the historical features that have situated the conceptual orientations of male and female athletes during the twentieth century. I suggest that how basketball players think is due to game rules and cultural expectations that have sanctioned particular patterns of bodily activity. In Chapters Two and Three I examine how court activity for the Iowa women culminated in a relational way of knowing that was a source of considerable agency, emotion, and knowledge. Relying on ritualized bodily activity and apprenticeship, players entered into a shared perceptual understanding unlike the conceptual orientation frequently required in their classrooms. In Chapter Four I describe how the lack of schematic portability across contexts of athletic and academic learning posed difficulties for some team members.

Documenting distinct sites of learning within a single institution, I hope this work will encourage the integration of institutional structures and the revision of policies that have traditionally splintered athletic and academic programming in many institutions. Unlike those who isolate athletic administrations for criticism, I analyze how various institutional domains preserve the ideological divide between mind and body, thereby denying the conceptual diversity of those who rely on this partnership to know. Challenging the assumption that language removes one from bodily constraints, I argue a need for academic instruction that minds the body by assisting students to draw on their situated experiences of being and knowing for the purposes of critical inquiry.

Notes

1. In 1987 the Presidents Commission sponsored an American Institute for Research (AIR) study that surveyed intercollegiate student athletes enrolled in forty-two of an existing 291 NCAA Division I schools. Based upon questionnaire and interview formats, the study represented the responses of 292 intercollegiate student athletes in high profile men's and women's sports. According to the AIR findings, 50 percent of those interviewed acknowledged a feeling that they lacked control of their academic lives. For an analysis of the study and its racial implications, see Hawkins (1995).

2. The concept of embodiment holds variable meaning across intellectual traditions that include *anthropology of the body* (Connerton 1989; Douglas 1966; Mauss 1973; Young 1994); *medicine and medical anthropology* (Damasio 1994, 1999; Grosz 1994; Komesaroff 1995; Lock and Scheper-Hughes 1987; Olson 1991; Rothfield 1995; Scheper-Hughes 1993; and Turner 1992); *cultural and feminist studies* (Bordo 1993; Butler 1993; Foucault 1984; Gallop 1995; O'Donovan-Anderson 1996); *phenomenology* (Csordas 1994; Merleau-Ponty 1962; Young 1990), and *cultural anthropology* (Abu-Lughod 1991). In this book, I consider embodiment a corporeal, cognitive, and cultural process. Unlike

some who focus exclusively on the influence of culture upon bodily image and activity, I expand the notion to include the influence of bodily activity upon thought. Located in, and shaped by, shifting ideological milieus, the body is the means by which concrete experiences enter into abstract mental structures that Mark Johnson (1987) terms "embodied schematic structures." These gestalts are distinct from those mental structures that emerge from symbolic activity. They are often responsible for significant affective and conceptual growth.

3. For a complete breakdown of graduation rates for Division I–III NCAA member institutions, see "1999 NCAA Graduation-Rates Summary" at www.ncaa.org/grad_rates.

4. John Hoberman (1997) challenges the assumption that sport in the United States has contributed to racial integration. He argues that "the cult of African American athleticism" has only reinforced racist assumptions about the intellectual achievement of African American males. While I agree with Hoberman's assertion that sport poses serious conceptual dilemmas for African American athletes, I reject his claim that African American males welcome, even cater, the images reserved for them. The racial and material inequities illustrated in Billy's case underscore his disdain for the stigma of athleticism.

Chapter One

The Transformation
of Space into Place

*But why was tackling necessary? ... It was because the men were al-
lowed to run with the ball and it was necessary to stop them. With
these facts in mind, I sat erect at my desk and said aloud: 'If he can't
run with the ball, we don't have to tackle; and if we don't have to
tackle, the roughness will be eliminated.' ... This time I felt that I
really had a new principle for a game, one that would not violate
any tradition.*

James Naismith, *Basketball:
Its Origin and Development* (1996)

*The goal of sociocultural research is to understand the relationship
between human mental functioning, on the one hand, and cultural,
historical, and institutional setting, on the other. ... It represents
one of the ways that psychology, anthropology, education, and related disciplines can take a new step in entering into public discourse
about today's most compelling issues.*

James Wertsch, "The Need for Action
in Sociocultural Research" (1995)

Having lived in various regions of the world, I have grown interested in
how the body and mind are shaped by their location in place. A decade
ago on Santorini, the southernmost island of the Greek Cycladic chain,
I weathered a storm with five traveling companions. Respite for us had
come in a local bar, where we befriended a villager who invited us to a

taverna on the island's far side. Warmed by ouzo, we embarked on borrowed Vespas, dodging the cavernous potholes that accompanied each pitch of our leader's taillight. A short time later, we arrived at the rural bodega where, inside, an aqueous haze of clove-scented cigarette smoke enveloped all but a stoic musician in a distant corner. The local farmers who listened bore expressions as austere as the hillside terraces they tended by day. Within minutes, I felt our entrance had been a mistake. Though only three of us were female, we were enough to infest this tightly woven cocoon of machismo. Stares, acute and scornful, said as much. The relationship of person to place seemed clear. By virtue of my body, I did not belong.

Anthropologist Yi-Fu Tuan (1977) maintains that the degree of connection one feels for a place has much to do with how "the body responds to such basic features of design as enclosure and exposure, verticality and horizontality, mass, volume, interior spaciousness, and light" (119). I maintain that how the body is *allowed* to respond in a place determines not just connection but thought. Recent scholarship in cultural geography underscores the consequential effect of place. In addition to traditional humanistic interest in the transformative potential of place (Buttimer 1993; Casey 1996; Entrikin 1991), cultural geographers have begun to document the experiences of exile and displacement, panoptism, environmental destruction, and reclamation, (Bodley 1988; Burger 1990; Gupta & Ferguson 1992) upon the bodies and minds of inhabitants. As James Wertsch (1995) suggests, those who document cognition as situated in human action must do so in the broadest sense, aware that specific practices of teachers and learners are themselves situated by cultural, historical, and institutional forces infiltrating the design and management of place. In this chapter, I consider how experiences of court space have shaped the knowledge of generations of learners. To understand the athletic learning of women in this study, one must return to the very origin of the game they played.

Legislating Place:
The Boundaries of Being and Knowing

During the fall and early winter of 1891, James Naismith struggled desperately to envision an indoor game that might engage his students. As a physical education instructor at the Young Christian Men's Association (YMCA) training school in Springfield, Massachusetts, he had been unable to interest students once cold temperatures necessitated that physical exercise take place indoors. Gymnastics and body building in the European tradition had been miserable failures. A day before

Naismith was expected to present his new game in a graduate seminar in which he was enrolled, he fell into despair.

> With weary footsteps I mounted the flight of narrow stairs that led to my office directly over the locker room. I slumped down in my chair, my head in my hands and my elbows on the desk. I was a thoroughly disheartened and discouraged young instructor. Below me, I could hear the boys in the locker room having a good time; they were giving expression to the very spirit that I had tried so hard to evoke. (1996, 43)

Despite his considerable doubt, Naismith devised a unique interior game. His thirteen rules for basketball sanctioned distinct patterns of mobility, space, time, and sensory engagement for those who played. From these legislated and recurring patterns of bodily activity emerged a conceptual orientation that would reflect Naismith's interest in collaborative play.

In *The Body in the Mind: The Bodily Basis of Meaning, Imagination, and Reason*, Mark Johnson (1987) insists that bodily activity is responsible for an array of "image" schemata that extend from concrete activity to guide abstract, even metaphorical, understanding. These mental structures are distinct from "propositional" structures that originate from symbolic activity. According to Johnson, the image schemata that originate in bodily activity are not distinct mental images but rather abstract structures that attune us to "causal relations, temporal sequences, part–whole patterns, relative locations, agent–patient structures, or instrumental relations" (28). Through a process Johnson terms "imaginative projection," these "embodied" schemata arise from bodily activity to play a central role in meaning and rationality.

As Naismith contemplated a winter game that would engage his students, he understood that interior space necessitated confinement. Setting boundaries on being, he established concrete limits on learners' experiences of "in" and "out." His earliest attempts at containment would prove difficult for students to accept. As he recalled,

> Early in the first half, the ball went into the gallery, and immediately the players from one team scrambled for the narrow stairway, crowding it so that they could make little speed. Two of the players on the other team, boosted one of the mates up until he could catch the lower part of the balcony, swing himself up, and regain the out-of-bounds ball. (1996, 67)

Johnson argues that one's sense for containment arises from concrete experiences of "in" and "out" and orients her to recognize and identify with distal or proximal conditions, even in an ideational realm. Johnson writes, "When we actually move from one place to another, we experience ourselves as traversing a path from one bounded area to another. This experience . . . provides a basis for our understanding of negation" (1987, 39). In effect, the recurring physical experience of being "inside" or "outside" culturally codified boundaries shapes an individual's abstract, or nonphysical, understanding of herself as actor or audience, accepted or negated, insider or outsider.

Unlike football and rugby, basketball demanded a heightened sense for containment. But spatial constraints created an additional problem—the temptation for players to initiate physical contact in such a confined site. By prohibiting contact and elevating the goal from a horizontal to a vertical plane, Naismith resolved the problem of force. Players' bodily activity was oriented less toward each other than toward two elevated goals on either end of the court. Legislating penalties for physical contact, Naismith's rules further discouraged the tactical use of physical force against isolated targets. Instead, his rules privileged the diffusion of interrelated bodies across the court with the objective synchronic motion. From the spherical equilibrium of the ball to the equal distribution of a standing player's weight to the synchronic motion of five players across court space, systemic balance was central. According to Johnson, the embodied schematic structure that orients players toward systemic balance has a profound effect not just upon activity but upon cognition. With recurring experiences of balance, an embodied mental structure arises that inclines one to recognize "balanced personalities, balanced views, balanced systems, balanced equations, the balance of power, the balance of justice, and so on" (Johnson 1987, 87).

Soon after Naismith introduced his game, spectators filled the gymnasium gallery for his physical education class. Additional restrictions on dribbling, passing, out-of-bounds play, and center jumping increased players' sense for containment and balance. Writing in 1941, Naismith recalled,

> Some teachers from the Buckingham Grade School were passing the gym one day, and hearing the noise, decided to investigate. They could enter the gallery through a door that led to the street. Each day after that, they stopped to watch the game, sometimes becoming so interested that they would not have time to get their lunch. These teachers came to me one day and asked me why girls could not play the game. I told them that I saw no reason why they could not, and this group organized the first girls' basketball team. (1996, 58)

Traditionally excluded from many sporting opportunities, females participated in basketball nearly from the beginning. Not unlike other cultural places, however, the insistence upon physiological differences resulted in a separate set of rules. In 1892, Senda Berenson, a physical education instructor at nearby Smith College, divided the court into three sections in which she ruled female players to stay.

Berenson's modifications insured the immobility of the female player for much of the next century. Rejecting Naismith's expanded notion of containment, which had allowed each player full access to the ball anywhere on the court, Berenson restricted female activity to particular portions of the floor. Two years later, Clara Gregory Baer, an instructor at Sophie Newcomb College in New Orleans, further confined female activity in her version of "basquette." According to Laura Bollig (1993),

> Baer's rules divide the court according to the number of players on a side—11 sections if 11 players. . . . No dribbling or guarding is allowed. A player is given six seconds to aim and shoot the ball. No backboards are allowed. Players may run only when the ball is in the air and then only a few steps within their area. (584)

In 1899 Dr. Luther Gulick, Naismith's former seminar professor in Springfield, appointed Berenson and four other women to the Women's Basketball Committee, entrusting them with the task of standardizing the game for girls and women. Berenson's three-court, limited-dribble game was adopted and its rules soon distributed by the Spalding Athletic Library.

The Berenson game foreshortened the space in which the female body was free to move. Discourses of femininity and masculinity evident in game rules resulted in gendered bodily activity that reinforced assumptions about the physiological deficiencies of girls and women. Occupying fixed positions on court, female players observed action when it passed beyond their midst. Diminished experiences of containment, verticality, and motion influenced the conceptual orientation of girls and women. In her phenomenological account of the female sporting body, Iris Marion Young (1990) explains,

> . . . feminine spatial existence is positioned by a system of coordinates that does not have its origin in her own intentional capacities. The tendency for the feminine body to remain partly immobile in the performance of a task that requires the movement of the whole body illustrates this characteristic of feminine bodily existed as rooted in place. (152–153)

The segmented floor and limited dribble denied female players the circumambient freedom Naismith had envisioned for boys and men. Unable to traverse between forward and rear space, female players acculturated to the court in the manner that characterized their stationary conduct in other cultural places. "Rooted" in place, girls and women had little opportunity to experience systemic balance. In the same manner that other cultural places allocated to females a distal condition, a splintered court removed learners from proximal connection to each other.

On a conceptual level, immobility of the body prevented female learners from achieving the kind of reflexive consciousness central to relational play. Unable to understand their play dialectically, players made mechanical contributions to a larger whole that no single player could fully experience in connection with an other. Donna Qualley (1997) explains reflexivity this way,

> Reflexivity is not the same thing as reflection, although they are often part of the same recursive and hermeneutical process. When we reflect, we fix our thoughts on a subject; we carefully consider it, meditate upon it. Self-reflection assumes that individuals can access the contents of their own mind independently of others. Reflexivity, on the other hand, does not originate in the self but always occurs in response to a person's critical engagement with an 'other.' Unlike reflection, which is a unidirectional thought process, reflexivity is a bidirectional, contrastive process. The encounter with an other results in new information or perspectives which we must hold up to our current conception of things. (11)

For male players, Naismith's game required the constant negotiation of bodily activity from which reflexive consciousness emerged. For those who possessed spatial license, systemic balance demanded that one understand his place through the perspectives of other players and in relation to an entire system of play. As Phil Jackson and Hugh Delehanty (1995) write in *Sacred Hoops*, "Basketball is a sport that involves the subtle interweaving of players at full speed to the point where they are thinking and moving as one. To do that successfully, they need to trust each other on a deep level and know instinctively how their teammates will respond in pressure situations" (1995, 17). Because Berenson's game prevented female players from thinking and moving as one, learners oriented to a conceptual orientation that emphasized one's reflective assessment of her isolated play.

Interestingly, the ideological and material influences upon court place for African American females were distinct from those Berenson's game enforced. Cindy Gissendanner (1994) notes that the "racial segregation, relatively low-class status, and the ideal of a more active femininity predisposed African American women as a group to reject the athletic model promoted by most white female physical educators" (81). According to Gissendanner, many African American and working-class women played Naismith's game in segregated schools and leagues, thereby circumventing the reforms of the women's Division of the National Amateur Athletic Federation (NAAF). From 1923 to 1940, this organization insisted that competitive sport threatened the physical welfare and reproductive capacity of females. As an alternative, the organization supported principles of leisure "play." Influential in middle-class communities, NAAF reforms led to declining competitive opportunities for white females. From 1920 to 1960, according to Gissendanner, the most competitive and liberating sporting opportunities belonged to African American and working-class females removed from the ideological influence of the NAAF. In the late 1930s in North Carolina, for instance, only African American female teams could compete for a state championship title, an opportunity unavailable to white players (Gissendanner 1994, 84). From more liberated forms of bodily activity, one might speculate that African American females fostered schematic orientations more akin to male players. Until civil rights legislation mandated the desegregation of public schools, many African American females continued to enjoy expanded experiences of containment, verticality, motion, and balance. Ironically, desegregation would introduce this constituency to the discursive and material inequities that had long shaped the activity of white females.

Regional Sanctions on the Experience of Place

In her historical review of high school girls' basketball in Iowa, Janice Beran (1993) suggests that for numerous reasons the reform efforts of the National Amateur Athletic Federation had little influence in that state. In the 1920s, an absence of physical educators espousing Federation principles allowed an organized group of Iowa school administrators and coaches to respond to the wishes of a primarily agrarian public that viewed competitive basketball as entirely appropriate for girls. The cultural orientation of the Iowa Girls High School Athletic Union (IGHSAU), founded in 1925, did not accept assertions that rigorous physical exercise jeopardized girls' health. According to Beran,

> Males working alongside females in the barns and fields knew that females were capable of exertion and that playing basketball would not cause them too much physical damage, and certainly not limit their reproductive capabilities as some leading educators and physicians were predicting. Players and their families paid little heed to their dour warnings. (1993, xiv)

Iowa union officials oversaw the continued existence of competitive sports for girls when programs in most states were dying in number. Prior to World War II, adaptations in the rules had brought about a two-court game in Iowa, thereby increasing the tempo of play and the mobility of the female body. Conceptually, this two-court game allowed limited opportunities for reflexive engagement. On their respective ends of the floor, defenses and offenses coordinated patterns of synchronic play. The game was popular and by 1947, seven-tenths of those girls in Iowa high schools played organized basketball (Beran 1993, 51).

Despite adaptations, the bodily activity of female players in Iowa was still largely determined by the discursive control of organizing officials, coaches, and journalists. Consciousness among players was bracketed by overarching cultural constraints placed on bodily display and comportment. Reporting for CBS news, Gene Schumate characterized the 1947 Iowa High School Girls State Tournament this way,

> . . . the most enjoyable phenomena year after year to the Hawkeye home folks is girls' basketball. And the ladies, bless 'em, get prettier as the years roll by. . . . The usual raiment consists of abbreviated shorts and snug blouses, loose only at the arm for free arm action. Most of the girls wear knee pads and shoes in a delicate shade that won't clash with the uniforms. Last year a coach's wife from Hartley— Mrs. O. E. Lester, designed and made uniforms for her girls. When they trotted out on the floor . . . they brought appreciative 'ohs' and a few whistles. The bare midriff uniform had bowed into high school basketball circles. . . . The states which do not permit girls high school basketball do so on the grounds that the competition would spoil a girl's sense of femininity. We can't agree with that in Iowa. We've taken to our hearts these lassies who play all out and race madly hither and yon but still remember to pause in the midst of a scoring rally to adjust a hair ribbon. We think it's the greatest show on earth. (qtd. in Beran 1993, 52)

Theorized from a broad sociocultural perspective, bodily activity even for rural players in Iowa configured according to the surveillance of those who demanded that their activity not threaten the supremacy of the male body. Still, overwhelming testimony from participants suggests that competitive sport, though restrictive from a contemporary standpoint, still allowed them a sense of agency otherwise unavailable (Beran 1993). What we recognize today with some cynicism was, within the context of the time, one of the only institutionalized opportunities for Iowa females to experience relational knowing. That restrictions upon the body mitigated against opportunities for reflexive engagement cannot completely discount the existence of agency. To the extent that these female participants defined themselves, they often felt they were defining much more. For Iowa towns decimated by demographic change and the ever-present threat of school consolidation, the success of local athletic teams bolstered a wavering sense of place.

Naismith's rules, reinterpreted over time, legislated particular ways of being and knowing. Discursive and material sanctions imposed upon female players did not begin to change until the passage of Title IX legislation in 1972, when secondary and post-secondary institutions were required by law to eliminate gendered restrictions in sites of athletic and academic learning. Growing up in one of the few Iowa communities to institute NAAF reforms, I would not have the opportunity to play competitive basketball until I reached high school, after nearly a decade of watching Iowa girls' basketball from the bleachers. For women in this study cultural constraints also existed. As Tangela explained, her athleticism posed a challenge to entrenched assumptions about female comportment. Even when she preferred not to, Tangela engaged in compensatory public performance, "dressing up fancy" so as to uphold the display of femininity she had jeopardized on the hardwood.

The Institutional Character of Carver-Hawkeye Arena

We talk every game about how this is our house and this is a sacred place. It's nice to be able to walk through that tunnel and see the black and gold and be able to feel the bright lights. That's a warm feeling.

Angie Lee

Home to numerous University of Iowa athletic programs, Carver-Hawkeye Arena is nestled west of the main campus amidst trees and occasional grouped blocks of native Iowa limestone. Unlike many athletic facilities that pronounce their sovereignty through multiple stories of sheer-faced concrete, Carver-Hawkeye exudes inordinate modesty. Constructed not by ascension but by submergence into the earth, the arena's single story seems benign, topped only by exterior air intake ducts and exposed ceiling supports that project a factory-like appearance not unfamiliar to those ticket holders who mind agrarian-based industries in Cedar Rapids, Dubuque, and the Quad Cities.

Once inside, I am always drawn across the upper concourse to an interior railing that affords me an unobstructed, expansive view. For a few moments, I soak in the golden sheen of the subterranean court, an island of polished wood parquet immersed in light. From this upper concourse, vertical descent to courtside is steep, frequently leaving fans with a vertigo that halts their progress midway up or down an aisle. In combination with the steep descent, an absence of section dividers and stair rails narrows the distance between player and audience. Unlike intricately sub-sectioned arenas elsewhere in the Big Ten Conference, Carver-Hawkeye fosters an intimacy between those who watch and those who play. The price for fans, in addition to the cost of entrance, is that they must negotiate hundreds of steps unassisted by architecture. I am well acquainted with the arena, able to descend without diverting my gaze from the parquet. Others, less familiar or more wary, invest considerably more concentration. Whatever the strategy, entering the navel of the arena makes one suddenly conscious of her body.

Prior to an institutional mandate that appropriately disallowed complimentary game tickets to academic tutors, I attended several men's basketball games, most of them during the 1986–1987 season when I supervised daily study table for the team. In mid-February, the Iowa men were undefeated and ranked number one in the Associated Press poll. On Valentine's Day 1987, Iowa hosted second-ranked Purdue. As a stultifying cold gripped much of the state, the gold-fringed parquet of Carver-Hawkeye radiated warmth, and I looked forward to watching the students with whom I worked.

To thwart Coach Gene Keady and the Purdue Boilermakers, the Hawkeyes would need to cultivate a confluence of mind in spite of the dizzying bombardment of sound that extinguished anything they attempted to say to one another. Throughout the game, unable to hear the players and coaches one row ahead of me, I could only feel. And what I felt was strange. Explosive waves of sonic energy plunged from ceiling to court, slamming into the parquet before reverberating upwards, palpably, from my feet to my head. For an entire game, sound shot to the floor, bearing down as if, somehow, those of us at the bottom of the cauldron could absorb it all. Inside the paint, players groaned as muscles wrenched against pressure, as loose elbows flew into tight jaws, as arm hacks stalled wrists and forearms without penalty. The experience was surreal to me and remains strange to this day. Not until this moment when I connected sight to sound did I fully appreciate the presence of force in the men's game.

For male and female players, Carver-Hawkeye fostered distinct ways of being and knowing. Among intercollegiate male student athletes in high-revenue sports, there exists considerable pressure not just to win but to garner the kind of individual attention that earns one attention in the professional draft. The increasing professionalization of intercollegiate men's basketball and football is evident in the exorbitant contracts, endorsements, and miscellaneous perquisites lavished upon those who coach. Such a climate inevitably shapes the conceptual orientation of those who play. As Billy acknowledges,

> We have a lot of players out there who are selfish. They don't care about the team. They only care about their own advancement. Sometimes I wonder, can you blame them?

Increasing public hunger for displays of individual prowess now disrupts the reflexive consciousness Naismith's game encouraged. Today, intercollegiate male student athletes learn under coaches who reap million dollar salaries and who exhibit little direct influence upon the academic welfare of those they bring to campus. The gross differentials in material worth that distinguish a head coach from his players do not escape the notice of many African American student athletes who, like Billy, are inclined to understand their physical "labor" by way of historical parallels.

What has changed for men during the past two decades, as corporate ideologies influence how players, coaches, and fans perceive the sport, is a heightened emphasis upon the conquest of individual players. Soliciting intercollegiate and professional shoe endorsements throughout the 1980s, Nike introduced a corporate marketing strategy that encouraged fans to purchase the footwear of those particular acrobats who game after game most capably slam-dunked their way to triple-digit victories. Since then, in seductive advertising and multiplying logos, merchandisers of athletic shoes and apparel have obliterated the aesthetic Naismith envisioned. In its place, a corporate ideology celebrates singular conquest. Today, the predominance of force schemata in the learning of males who participate in high profile, intercollegiate sports constitutes the normative athletic experience for fans and critics alike. While Billy understood himself as powerless, his embodiment of force on the football field certainly opened him to the criticism of those who resented his proximity to material privilege. In this way, male student athletes in high revenue sports are subject to criticism in a way that female student athletes are not. Regardless of how he understood himself, or how isolation in an athletic enterprise undercut his academic involvement, Billy was subject to the scrutiny of those who resented expression of force and his connection to economic power.

In his discussion of the "professionalization of sport," philosopher Joseph Kupfer (1995) suggests that fans have relinquished an "aesthetic attitude," an appreciation of sport in terms of rhythms, movements, and symmetries. It may be that women's intercollegiate basketball attracts those fans who regret fundamental ideological shifts that threaten the reflexive consciousness Naismith's game encouraged for much of this century. Today, the original emphasis upon systemic balance typifies the play of female student athletes while the men's game increasingly attunes itself to force.

Unlike most women's athletic programs in the country, female student athletes at the University of Iowa at the time of this study were members of an autonomous women's athletic department administered largely by women who had participated actively in gender equity legislation and for whom the defining moment for Hawkeye women's basketball remained February 3, 1985, when 22,175 people jammed Carver-Hawkeye for an Iowa-Ohio State women's contest. Surpassing a previous arena attendance record for a men's basketball game by the thousands, as well as breaking existing fire codes, fans braved the cold in a show of allegiance that astounded even the most optimistic members of the women's athletic program.

For head coach C. Vivian Stringer, the crowd fulfilled a professional vow to sell out Carver-Hawkeye Arena. In 1984, Stringer had become the first African American head coach in the history of women's athletics at the University of Iowa. Formerly head coach at Cheyney State, a predominantly African American college located near Philadelphia, she had "cemented her reputation for making the most out of little and settling for nothing short of the best from her players and herself" (Smith 1995, 25). In short order at Iowa, Stringer, and athletic director Dr. Christine Grant had created a distinctive cultural place for female student athletes. The architecture of Carver-Hawkeye Arena offers palpable evidence of equity among men's and women's athletic programs. Team lounges, used for meetings and game tape sessions, as well as adjacent dressing facilities, are similar in feature, design, and dimension for both men's and women's basketball teams. Less than a three hour drive from Iowa City, the situation at Iowa State University, a sister institution, has until recently been considerably different. In the early 1990s, nearly a decade after Carver-Hawkeye's construction, the Office of Civil Rights found ISU guilty of a series of Title IX violations, including gender discrepancies in travel allowances, pregame housing, locker rooms, and recruiting budgets (Grant and Curtis 1995, 2). Located within a single athletic administration, women's programs at Iowa State reflected inequities that a relatively independent administration at the University of Iowa had challenged and overcome.

By the time of this study, female basketball players oriented to a contemporary game much like the original version Naismith created for males. Forwards contributed verticality and muscle while guards lent their speed, range, and motion. From 5:30 to 8:30 AM each morning of the season, players and coaches occupied the court in solitude. How they learned and how, in turn, they understood themselves led to a reflexive orientation unlike conceptual orientations available to preceding generations of female players. Still, while members of the 1995 team were beneficiaries of an institutional commitment to gender equity in sport, they did not experience Carver-Hawkeye Arena without struggle. Though players engaged in activity that welcomed bodily difference, they did not escape broader cultural expectations for female comportment and display. During athletic contests, players shared court space with male and female cheerleaders who were uniformly white and nearly identical in height, weight, appearance, and activity. Each female cheerleader was lifted, thrown, and caught by a male partner who was hers for the season. Fringed by these monogamous white performers, the Iowa women—from point guard to power post—moved together in ways distinct from gendered practices enacted on the sidelines. Sensitive to these competing embodiments, one understands Carver-Hawkeye Arena as both dynamic and static. Public performances were multi-layered "contests" in which place was an event, a single moment in a broader historical struggle for more liberatory ways of being and knowing.

One of the most significant contributions of research in situated cognition is its attention to how the relation of mind and activity is shaped by sociohistorical forces that preexist and predetermine learners. According to Valerie Walkerdine (1997), "Situated cognition . . . is not people thinking in different contexts, but subjects produced differently in different practices . . . " (65). Seen in this way, the production of knowledge is always itself a production of history. Considering the conceptual orientation of generations of learners, this chapter suggests how shifts in bodily activity specifically affected the thoughts of those who played. How the female sporting body was legislated over time altered not just bodily activity but, in turn, the nature of learners' conceptual orientation. Though inequities constrained female play for much of the twentieth century, gradual regard for Title IX legislation altered the nature of bodily activity for girls and women. With more liberatory experiences of motion, verticality, and balance, females had the opportunity to synchronize their bodies in a way that made reflexive consciousness possible.

Chapter Two

The Pursuit
of Systemic Balance

*Once you sign that paper you're bonded to the women's basketball
team. I thank God for sending me here because I continue to grow.
There are a lot more sisters on the team. I put myself in positions, or
I find myself in positions, where I see my sisters, either Black or white.*
Nadine Domond

*To be successful, a team must perform many skills and play options
well. It must also be lucky, which means avoiding injury or sickness
at critical times over the season or getting the "breaks" during games.
The cornerstone of success, however, is having clearly defined goals
that all members agree on and commit themselves to achieving. This
commitment to a mutually shared purpose sustains all members of
the team through the difficulties, the challenges, and the heartbreak
of a season of competitive basketball. This commitment also enables
them to put the welfare of the team ahead of their own.*
Vic Pruden, *A Conceptual
Approach to Basketball* (1987)

The interdisciplinary field of performance studies has been centrally
concerned with the dialectical relation of place and human activity.[1] In
his analysis of the historical development of the Western theater stage,
Richard Schechner (1988) considers how the modern proscenium reflects ideological and material interest in concealment and control. He
suggests, in contrast, that the early Greek amphitheater was a site that

allowed fluid and emergent relationships between actor and audience. Schechner analyzes the open and intimate design of classical amphitheaters for their conceptual effect, noting how the design of place allowed for bodily activity that, in turn, influenced participants' connection to polis. Schechner's work underscores how inhabitants' activity can transform the experience of place. Of interest to Schechner are those sites that stimulate rather than stymie cultural invention. He describes them as social creases,

> Creases are places to hide, but more importantly they signal areas of instability, disturbance, and potentially radical changes in the social topography. Even in large, apparently smooth operations like corporations and universities, creases exist; look for them, quite literally, in "out of the way places." (1988, 164)

Across a host of disciplines, researchers have begun to analyze the capacity of human activity to alter the experience of place. In her own work among the Liberian Vai, anthropologist Jean Lave (1997) documented features of apprenticed learning in "communities of practice." While Lave shares Valerie Walkerdine's (1997, 1998) interest in situated cognition, she emphasizes the formative rather than the productive function of activity. From an analysis of place that documents how shifting bodily practices "produced" generations of female basketball players, this chapter acknowledges Lave's view that, through certain forms of activity, human beings can alter not just their relationships but their knowledge making. In the tradition of this research, this chapter considers how coaches and players experienced the court as a site of transformative activity.

Apprenticeship and the Politics of Perception

Of the many dilemmas that face a head coach, perhaps the most challenging is coming not just to gauge the learning histories that freshman players bring to the court each season but, in quick order, to teach the conceptual orientation already embodied in the minds of upper class learners. The desired outcome is a steady progression of a team through three realms of consciousness,

> At the lowest level, the players' thoughts and actions are not governed by a system of play. Although the players may adhere to the rules of the game and display the beginnings of organized play, their play is more a function of aggressiveness, athletic ability, and individual initiative than an overall plan. Although some players may exhibit readiness and one-on-one skills, very little evidence is shown of any sophisticated team play. At the middle level of consciousness, players are aware of a

> system of play. At times, the system may be very sophisticated indeed. At this level, however, the system is personified in the coach. The players, therefore, know the system only through their coach. Their relationship is somewhat like that of the puppeteer and the puppets. The thoughts and actions of the player during the course of play are governed . . . by their coach. At the highest level of consciousness . . . players know and understand a system of play that they have agreed to follow. In a game . . . the players are free to use their imagination and creativeness . . . provided that their movement and actions are consistent with their system of play. (Pruden 1987, 102)

Achieving the third level of consciousness requires that players commit to a shared "system of play." To this end, each player, regardless of her status on the team, must feel herself to be a participant. The third level of consciousness is highlighted by periods of intense and euphoric freedom among players on the court. Described by players as "flow" or "being in the zone," these stretches of play are the outcome learners seek. The definitive feature of a superior team is the ability of players and coaches to invoke the highest level of consciousness across an entire season of play.

The bodily activity that characterized learning for the Iowa women was a product of asymmetrical relations between the coach as teacher, older players as master students, and younger players as apprentices. Each position on the court required particular conceptual schemata, yet the prerequisite to successful play demanded that players operate in a "relational matrix" (Becker 1995) that defied individualism. Players understood that relational knowing required one to move beyond positional knowledge to a deeper sense for all options possible at the other four positions on court. Jenny, a junior reserve center, explained the string metaphor that Coach Lee used to encourage collective consciousness.

> Coach Lee teaches guards the "string concept." You're not supposed to get closer than maybe ten or twelve feet. When this person cuts through, you stay on the string. If she cuts away from you, she's pulling you with her. If she cuts over there, you don't stay over here because if she's stuck, she can't pass the ball back to you. . . . After you've been playing with the same people for a while, you almost start to get on the same brain waves. It's comfortable. You get really confident and, "Well, yeah, they understand. They understand what I'm thinking, and I understand what they're thinking." I can lob a pass up to Tan and expect her to catch it. I know her timing on her jump and how high she is going to jump or if she is going to be up higher in the lane when she posts. I think that's what makes a team really successful. If you know that person is going to be there without even having to look at them. You can always depend on them being there. . . . If you can't expect this person to do this, then you . . . "Well, yester-

day you cut out to the wing and today you're cutting up to the top. Well, which way is it? I don't know what to expect with you." You don't know how to deal with it. Once you start playing with a person you understand their moves. You understand what they're thinking.

Only by "being there" together in body did players enter into relational knowing. For Jenny and her teammates, bodily activity was the means to a collective mindset. To this end, learning was necessarily a political process in which coaches and elder players assisted novices to acquire embodied understanding. As this chapter will show, younger players may be unwilling to relinquish the orientations they bring to the court. Or, coaches and master students may dictate rather than model and teach. Each season, a teacher and her elder learners must initiate associational shifts, supporting not just team goals and skill-making but escorting younger players through activity to understanding.

Though not the first Hawkeye women's basketball coach, C. Vivian Stringer's twelve-year tenure, which ended the summer before my fieldwork, included a stunning list of accomplishments: six Big Ten Championships, ten NCAA tournaments bids, a Final Four appearance, and three All-American players. In the end, however, Coach Stringer can hardly be remembered apart from the struggles that characterized her final years at Iowa, unusual seasons when the seepage of personal into professional took its toll. In November 1992, the sudden death of Stringer's husband left her a single mother of three children. During that turbulent season, players experienced a heightened state of crisis. When Stringer took a mid-season leave of absence, an assistant took her place, and the team entered into what Victor Turner (1969) calls a "liminal" condition "betwixt and between" the structure of what had been and the anti-structure of what loomed.[2] In the wake of Stringer's departure, players who formally relied on their head coach as the mind behind their individual play now faced a perceptual crisis, one that intensified with subsequent deaths of a ball girl, a team doctor, and a player's father. Each tragedy reintroduced the possibility of disintegration, reawakening what Phil Carpsecken (1993) describes as the "ontological suspicion that one may really in fact 'be nothing,' . . . that a void does indeed underlie all the world we work to construct and maintain" (297–298).

During this tenuous period, I frequently stopped to observe team practices before tutoring sessions at Carver-Hawkeye Arena. What seemed apparent as the conference season progressed was a dramatic shift in how players associated with each other as they learned. Refusing with their coach's prolonged absence and each subsequent tragedy to "be nothing," elder players seemed to take considerable responsibility for facilitating the perceptual process of younger players. Of this negotiation, Nick Crossley (1996) writes,

> . . . as no two people can occupy the same place at the same time, they
> will not necessarily see the same things. Indeed there are many factors
> which might account for discrepancies in visual experiences, ranging
> from social position and 'cultural capital' through purpose, mood, and
> momentary inclination. All of these factors may lead us to interrogate
> our environment differently. . . . Perceivers can argue and debate
> about what they see and can show and teach each other to see the
> same things in the same ways. They can enter into each other's per-
> ceptual fields. (30)

While assistant coaches supervised this negotiation, elder players
seemed to assume responsibility for consulting teammates before
and after drills. The suspension of previous roles and responsibilities allowed players to recalibrate their perception. From liminality
emerged *communitas*, which Victor Turner (1969) describes as "almost
everywhere held to be sacred or 'holy,' possibly because it transgresses
or dissolves the norms that govern structured and institutionalized
relationships and is accompanied by experiences of unprecedented
potency" (128).

Once Stringer returned, she observed practices without interrupting in the manner and frequency of her previous teaching. She seemed
to assume the position of learner, subordinating her role in ways that
necessitated players' continued leadership. Where she had taken primary responsibility for orchestrating the perceptual process early in the
season, she seemed to recognize the capacity of players to teach themselves. By the early spring of that season, associational adjustments
among players and coaches had contributed to a string of victories that
culminated in a National Collegiate Athletic Association (NCAA) regional final game against the University of Tennessee. Hosting the game,
the Hawkeyes had an opportunity to knock this perennial Southeastern Conference favorite out of the tournament and proceed to the
women's NCAA Final Four in Atlanta. During the week preceding the
contest, the local and state press seemed decidedly aloof. The reputation of the Tennessee Lady Volunteers under head coach Pat Summitt
had convinced many that the Iowa Hawkeyes would be unable to defend their home. Experienced champions, the Lady Vols had seized national titles in 1987, 1989, and 1991. Karen Clayton, a freshman point
guard for Iowa that season, would later remember the contest as her favorite game, despite the fact she never left the bench.

> I could watch it over and over again. I have the tape. It was great. Just
> the feeling. It was the weirdest thing, but you could feel we were go-
> ing to win. We had that feeling, "So what they're Tennessee? So what?"
> You could feel it. Definitely.

Looking back, Karen understood the regional final as the highlight of
her athletic career. As she noted, the Iowa players were hardly fazed by

the Lady Vols. They had long before assumed control of their learning. Defeating Tennessee, the Hawkeyes would proceed to their first Final Four appearance.

Two years later, during the 1994–1995 season, I would begin tutoring Tangela, one of seven bluechip recruits local media lauded as the "Sensational Seven." In the wake of early defeats, tension escalated between novices and elder players, those women who remembered the associational adjustments that had secured victories two years earlier. In *Dramas, Fields, and Metaphors,* Victor Turner (1974) notes that "The neophyte in liminality must be a *tabula rasa,* a blank slate on which is inscribed the knowledge and wisdom of the group" (103). At the heart of the conceptual disarray Tangela's first season seemed the formidable contingent of freshmen who rejected the subordinate role expected of them, as well as the inability of master players to influence perception. Several years later Tangela would recall,

> . . . we [the freshmen] thought we were all that. Everybody wanted to be the leading scorer. The team had meetings. Tia was the captain, and she was telling us about team unity. And we probably weren't listening. We really didn't know the seniors. That was the conflict. We didn't know how to play with them.

In her final days at Iowa, C. Vivian Stringer conceded that she had lost the spirit to teach at Iowa. The strain was apparent not just to Stringer but to those who had watched her grow more lifeless with each game and press conference. In the summer of 1995, she resigned. Her successor would inherit a program in the midst of heightening expectations for what the Sensational Seven would do and become. As individuals, these women had led their respective high school teams to successful seasons. Yet a fundamental question remained. Would they invest in the health and sustenance of the team as a collective unit, or would the negotiation of meaning remain problematic?

Orchestrating the Big Payback

> At practices, the coach is a teacher. To fulfill this role [she] must create a learning environment that will help players to perform to their fullest powers of heart, spirit, will, intellect, and body. In this environment, [she] should help players by (a) making them "free," (b) involving them in their own learning, and (c) painting the big picture for them.
>
> Vic Pruden, *A Conceptual Approach to Basketball* (1987)

Stringer's departure created yet another liminal state. Because changes in offensive and defensive systems often lead to initial periods of deteriorated performance for learners, the Iowa players worried about a new head coach who might demand dramatic changes in bodily activity. On the heels of an 11–17 season and dreading the thought of another losing season, players unanimously supported the candidacy of Iowa assistant coach Angie Lee. As a senior at the University of Iowa in 1983 to 1984, Lee had been starting point guard and captain during Stringer's first season. For nine years Lee had served as Stringer's dogged assistant, and with Stringer's endorsement, as well as the mandate of the team, she was selected by a search committee who deemed continuity and character their primary criteria. As an assistant during the treacherous 1994–1995 season, Lee had observed the perceptual disintegration. She seemed to understand that problems of association did not necessarily warrant any changes in *what* players learned. Though she would loosen offensive and defensive formations, emphasize the fast break, and shorten practices, Lee would keep Stringer's play patterns largely intact. What players appreciated about Lee was her distinct blend of humor and intensity. While Stringer had focused upon the geometry of basketball, teaching the intricacies of angles and arcs, Lee was often described as "a player's coach," someone firm in her convictions but open to the inventiveness of players.

In late November 1995, I began attending daily practices, breakfasts, and games. Prior to my arrival, one member of the Sensational Seven had withdrawn from the university, returning to her home in California. Through the duration of the 1995–1996 season, I heard the player mentioned within my earshot on only two occasions. In time, I understood that the resilience of a team, its ability to endure over time, demands that players and coaches commit themselves to an intense experience of reciprocity. Such a compact did not allow the young women I observed to think beyond the immediacy of individual and collective need. On the occasions I asked a player or coach about the departing teammate, I always heard the same response. She had been unhappy and decided to leave. Whether or not Stringer's departure or Lee's arrival had precipitated this player's transfer I never came to know.

Lee's coaching style during her first season involved constant negotiation with players. Early that fall, she allowed team members to take an active role in marketing decisions. Nadine and Tangela recommended that the campaign headline the season as "The Big Payback." As Tangela explained,

> Nadine and I were talking. . . . And I remembered in high school when I played against Marshall . . . We broke their thirteen-year winning streak for the city championship. So, they came in our house and played "The Big Payback" on us. And I hated that song from then on.

So I was like, "Man, we should use 'The Big Payback' for our team!" I
don't know why, but I just wanted it to be like that. I thought about
the little poster idea and everything.

Promotional posters proclaimed 1995–1996 the year of "The Big Payback." And James Brown's rendition became a pregame ritual, as did a
ceremonial "payback count." Teams that had knocked off the Iowa
women in 1994–1995 were identified in order of their return in 1995–
1996. Each week, at the top of the locker room chalkboard, the team's
next target appeared as "Payback #1," "Payback #2," and so on. For
every loss the preceding year, the need for a payback was clear. Sensitive to the histories and desires of her players, Coach Lee allowed for
ritual innovations that became centrally important to how the team
conceptualized its purpose, thereby facilitating, to some degree, a succession of wins that few had anticipated. In short order, "payback" became a predominant theme in the rhetoric of players, coaches, fans,
and journalists.

In addition to honoring players' invention of rituals, Angie Lee engaged in exhaustive day-by-day analyses of nearly every player. Despite a familiarity she might have taken for granted, Lee took singular
interest in players' questions and concerns, making time for them after
practice and throughout the day and evening. Listening to how players
characterized their learning, Lee often responded with adjustments in
her coaching style. Referring to the first several months of the season
when she was struggling on the court, Jenny explained Lee's approach
this way.

> We had a really deep discussion. I pretty much talked about how I deal
> with things and how I've learned to deal with myself and my expec-
> tations. She [Coach Lee] said she's been giving me room, stepping
> back. She's like, "Don't think because I haven't really been getting on
> you as much lately . . . " I noticed that she was kind of getting on me
> and then she just stopped. And she's like, "Don't take that as I've given
> up on you. Don't think that at all." The coaches have learned how I
> deal with things. They stepped back and let me realize, "Oh, duh, I'm
> supposed to be topside. God, I know I'm supposed to X-step. I know
> I'm supposed to do this!" They realize that I learn from my mistakes,
> and I repeat things they've said over and over in my head.

Eventually, Jenny would pull out of her shooting slump. That Coach
Lee had negotiated this rough stretch of learning remained important
to her. That Jenny had been willing to acknowledge her frustrations
and thoughts to a coach who inevitably decided and assessed playing
time seemed equally significant.

Pain: The Intersection of Body, Mind, and Culture

> . . . pain leads its existence mostly in secret, in silence, without leaving written records or eloquent testimony. Our main evidence in documenting the historical life of pain lies in fragmentary episodes and in scattered moments.
>
> David Morris, *The Culture of Pain* (1991)

In early December I began to sense the conflictual nature of participatory learning for players and coaches. Early in the season, Simone Edwards, a 6'4" post player, had returned from a knee injury the previous season to average 7.4 points and 6.2 rebounds per game. In a nonconference tournament at the University of Kansas, Simone was named to the all-tournament team, playing a central role in the Hawkeye's defeat of #13 Kansas in the final game. Iowa players, coaches, and fans could not have been happier. During the previous season, Simone had assumed responsibility for energizing fans at a time when she might understandably have given up hope. Immobilized by a knee brace, she would stand for much of games, turning to spectators and, with the wave of a towel, single-handedly bring them to their feet. Now, the fall of 1995, Simone seemed finally to experience recompense for her selflessness. The week after her triumph at Kansas, however, Simone collapsed during a contest at Drake University. She had reinjured her anterior cruciate ligament (ACL), the connecting tissue stabilizing the central and forward portion of the knee. A few days later, exploratory surgery would reveal that torn cartilage had compounded the trauma. Simone's senior season came to an end just games after it had begun.

In the wake of such a serious injury, any partnership of mind and body a player has fostered begins to unravel. An injury victim recedes from the center of play to the periphery according not just to the gradation of her injury but to the response of teammates and coaches. In other words, pain is a physical *and* cultural construct. Nancy Scheper-Hughes (1993) suggests that "the structure of individual and collective sentiments down to the feel of one's body is a function of one's position and role in the technical and productive order" (185). For Billy, a player marginalized by persistent injury, pain had passed unacknowledged within the technical and productive order that was NCAA Division I football. In fact, across the contexts of Billy's learning, pain was constructed as a distinctly physical phenomenon relevant only to medical doctors and team trainers. Such an ideological view allowed the technical orders of sport and school to function without interruption. To athletic and academic personnel alike, Billy's pain was his own. In Simone's case, her altered location in the context of activity engendered a different conception of pain, inspiring personal *and* collective crisis. Simone's sudden absence introduced the prospect of momentary disintegration for team members and coaches. Though Simone had only just returned to play after an initial ACL tear, her healing had bolstered teammates who had cause to doubt their own resistance to injury.

To understand how bodily activity influences cognition, one must accord special attention to pain, an experience that often interrupts the relation of mind and body. One must also accept David Morris's (1991) view that "pain is never the sole creation of our anatomy and physiology. It emerges only at the intersection of bodies, minds, and cultures" (3). In this way, pain is a window not just to the tenuous relation of body and mind but to the fragile relation of individual and collective. In the pages that follow, I return to the team practice when I first recognized how Simone's injury held significance for her peers and teachers.

Simone's Legacy: A Team Rebuilds

December 12, 1995

I awake to the succession of alarms I have set for 4:30, 4:35, and 4:40 AM, three respectively. Nearly two weeks after the start of fieldwork, I find that I still require a three-alarm call to consciousness. I have had the sense to station my clocks in a line en route to the bathroom where, this morning, I deactivate a hostile Big Ben before it explodes on the medicine cabinet. I breathe a sigh of relief, aware that nothing is quite so uncivil as a clock that cannot distinguish grogginess from deep sleep. In the predawn, I dress for the day, choosing nylon sweats in teal, a navy scoop t-shirt, and cross-trainers, an outfit that wins me curious looks during the academic day but is requisite attire in the community of learners I join every morning for four hours. With just enough time to fill a large thermal cup with coffee, I depart, solaced by images of the gluttony that will accompany breakfast in four hours. Chef Jim Esch's training table is renowned among players, coaches, and staff. A gregarious consumer for slightly less than a week, I am still barely acquainted with a buffet that includes scrambled eggs, cubed potatoes, grits, sausages and bacon, casseroles (on a good day, homemade noodle), pancakes, toast, rolls, fruit, and juices.

The engine of my aged Nissan Sentra pulls and tugs as I exit the driveway, telltale signs of transmission failure that I dismiss in the hope that the car will live through the basketball season. I remind myself that I can worry about only so much these days. Fieldwork has created a state of perpetual exhaustion. Days that begin at 4:30 AM necessitate sleep at hours that promise an end to life as a social experience. Minutes away from Carver-Hawkeye Arena, I drive past the state's tertiary care facility, a sprawling conglomerate of hospitals, clinics, and schools constituting one of the largest university-owned medical training centers in the world. Schools of nursing, medicine, and dentistry are represented by a motley assortment of buildings, each testifying to a distinct architectural ontogeny that seems bent on subjugating earlier epochs. At 5:20 AM all is quiet. The shifts in hospital staff will not take place for another hour. I am glad to forego the obligatory peripheral search for white-coated doctors and residents who dart across these streets with little apparent regard for their own mortality.

Approaching Carver-Hawkeye, I find the ceiling lights still extinguished. From the parking lot I enter the upper concourse of Hawkeye Arena, where I locate the elevator that delivers me to ground floor. From the elevator I proceed to the "tunnel," the main artery connecting the court proper to an adjacent ground floor of team lounges and locker rooms; visitors' locker rooms; press, weight, and hospitality rooms; a towel and equipment area; a facilities office; and a rear service entrance. On game day, for players and coaches, the soundproof tunnel is a pathway to sensation. From the locker room to the court, they shoot into light, sound, and color.

It is now 5:40 AM. Having arrived twenty minutes ago, players are nearly finished dressing. Those who reside in Slater Dormitory have been delivered to the arena in a university van driven by the youngest of four student-managers. Players who reside off-campus must find their own way to the arena and park in a lot just outside the upper concourse. At 8:00 AM, the onset of metered hours, the freshman manager will scoop up quarters that players have provided her before practice and scurry to the lot, where she will fill the meters of cars licensed "Noll#55" and "EbonyIs." This year seven of twelve players reside in Slater. Of the remaining five, three share an apartment.

While players dress and coaches meet in a second-floor office to prepare for practice, I venture to the training room, where I know I will find life. Roxann, the head trainer, and her two student assistants are readying treatment supplies and equipment. Malikah is the first to enter, barefoot with socks and Reebok high-tops in hand. She is quiet and in a flat tone tells Roxann, "I want an MRI. I want to know what's wrong."

A victim last year of an anterior cruciate ligament tear, Malikah is clearly shaken by Simone's surgery. Single and multiple ligament injuries of the knee require extensive rehabilitation and often end athletic careers. Knowing all that from first experience, Malikah demands the only examination she believes will foretell her own future. But magnetic resonance imaging (MRI), a high-tech diagnostic procedure, has its price.

"Do you know how much that costs?" Roxann responds.

I ask Malikah about the MRI as Roxann leaves for the supply room, "Would that tell you about damage in your knee?"

"Sometimes it does. With my earlier one it did."

Malikah seems bothered that Simone had undergone rehabilitation last year without subsequent MRIs, which cost roughly $1,000 apiece.

"She didn't know what she was playing with. I don't want that to happen with me. I don't want to play that bad. She's only a couple months ahead of me [in the rehabilitation process]."

Festering in Malikah's mind is the realization that 6'4" center Simone Edwards is lost for her senior season, which means her career, a fact hardly believable given just a week ago she had been named a member of an all-tournament team. For her teammates and coaches, Simone had promised stability inside the paint. This morning, though, Malikah and her teammates know that Simone's arthroscopic surgery revealed ligament and, additionally, cartilage damage. Only 10 percent of her ACL remains intact. In effect, Simone's leg is held together at the knee by nothing more than a string of ligament, a stunning blow for someone who has already spent a medical redshirt year undergoing extensive and excruciating rehabilitation. A stunning blow for those who have watched Simone struggle toward recovery. As Coach Lee had remarked to the press, "It's very, very disappointing to see this happen. The way Simone worked to rehab the knee and to see this happen. . . . It just doesn't seem like anything's fair."

As I watch Roxann and Malikah, I, too, think of Simone. I recall practices of the past three days, purgatorial days between the reinjury and the exploratory surgery that propelled Simone into silence. One particular practice she had slipped out of the training room to watch her teammates play. On the sidelines, immobilized by an ankle to upper thigh brace, Simone sat alone until a break in action brought Coach Lee to her side. Coach Lee had appealed to Simone, "I know you want to be out there. You just gotta concentrate on what's ahead, what you can do." I was near enough to hear Lee's words. That Simone was near enough in spirit to comprehend them seemed a whole different question. Removed from her teammates in activity and perception, Simone's immobility is at once physical, psychical, and cultural. Now, Simone's absence seems also to immobilize her teammates, who no longer learn with or through her.

As other players begin to join Malikah in the training room, I think back to another moment in the last several days, an occasion when the team had gathered in the locker room to review the Drake game tape. Coach Lee had just finished noting the distinction between defensive recoveries that involve merely lunging and those that more adroitly slide when slowly the tape advanced toward the moment of Simone's injury. The room fell quiet as we observed Karen begin the lob pass that would soar just beyond Simone's grasp. When the tape captured Karen releasing the fateful lob, Simone lowered her head and closed her eyes. Jenny, sitting next to Simone on the lounge sofa farthest from the television monitor, wrapped her right arm around Simone's shoulder. Later, joining me in the arena seats after practice, Jenny would admit, "Sometimes it's hard to understand God's reasons."

Now, the morning after Simone's surgery, Malikah waits on a cushioned treatment table for Roxann to return, at which point the MRI debate continues. Roxann is polite but firm. Malikah's situation doesn't warrant such an expensive procedure. Her knee is different than Simone's.

"You don't have swelling like Simone did," Roxann notes. There is a pause in the conversation.

"All right," Malikah retorts, "I want some ice."

Roxann smiles and replies, "I want this. I want that." She leaves to fetch ice. Malikah is straight-faced, grim.

I continue to stand beside the treatment table upon which Malikah waits. Two bags of ice, taped tightly to her right knee with cellophane wrap, begin to take effect. The ice pack on her left knee fights recurring tendinitis. For both knees, the cold deadens sensitivity to the twists, the acceleration, and the jarring that constitute daily practice on hardwood. Malikah tells me that she called her mother last night, worried about her own injury. She recounts the somber aura of Simone's hospital room when doctors brought word that the reinjury was far worse than expected.

Shannon enters the training room, followed next by Karen, Tangela, and Angie. Tangela complains about the stained socks she has been given for practice. In minutes, eight players find their places on available treatment tables. The injury list is extensive. Shannon struggles with chronic shin splits, which a male trainer now helps her to stretch. For a healing hamstring, Shannon sports a heating pad. For her flu, she merely endures. Karen suffers the effects of a back injury incurred in a game last year. Now, eleven months later, she receives multiple therapies. When the pain requires it, Karen tapes two electrodes to either side of her lower back and at 30-minute intervals activates an electrode stimulation device the size of a small transistor radio. The therapy provides light electric stimulation to affected muscles. Amy stretches out next to Karen. She is a freshman with limited collegiate experience. Relatively healthy, she experiences only a bit of tendonitis in the right knee and a jammed left pinkie, which is taped. Tiffany Gooden, another ACL victim, recovers as does Malikah. Her knees experience chronic pain, for which—before and after practice—she is treated with ice.

Tangela suffers from plantar fasciaitis and tendinitis in the shoulder. Expressionless, she slides onto a treatment table, asking one of the assistants to begin massaging and taping her strained foot muscle. A stocky, blond-haired student responds and, since he has just begun his rotation with women's basketball, asks Tangela to identify the problem foot. Turning onto her stomach, Tangela curls her right leg back, then lifts herself, rising off her stomach to more precisely point to the spot. "Right there," she says flatly. In a few minutes Doug will prepare the electrode therapy for Tangela's right shoulder. In anticipation, she lifts her t-shirt above her sports bra so electrodes may be applied to the skin adjacent to her stressed rotator cuff. That done, she puts on her headphones, closes her eyes, and begins listening to a CD.

Angie continues to suffer a mysterious ankle injury, a hypersensitive sprain that has Roxann stumped. Nerves around the site of an ankle injury react to touch and light massage as though they were violent rubbings on the bone itself. With her injured leg dangling in the whirlpool, Angie slumps over my newest copy of the *Voice of the Hawkeyes*. The publication is produced weekly from September through November, bi-weekly from December through March, and monthly from April through August. For hungry Hawkeye fans, it offers feature articles, editorial commentaries, and sports news related to the university's athletic programs. The "voice" belongs to someone exclusively interested in football, wrestling, and men's basketball. Women's basketball receives token coverage, one feature article and one editorial response per issue.

Two latecomers enter the training room. Susan rests on a treatment table, sick with a bronchial infection that resists antibiotics. Nadine, sleeping on what was formerly Angie's treatment table, receives little attention. She is beginning to feel sick and Roxann admits there is not much to be done about that. I scan the training room and detect in injury and illness the exhaustion that escorts players through the course of a season.

At 5:55 AM, the players complete their treatments, raising themselves off tables to pull on socks and tie high-top Reeboks before departing the training room. Stacy trudges toward the arena, in step to her own whistled rendition of the theme song to *The Bridge over River Kwai*. I follow the group into the arena, which is now fully ablaze. Approaching the court, I see that all the players sit on the folding bench seats that are theirs during home games. They talk quietly but, in the main, just sit and stare. No one stretches or shoots as usual. Roxann and I find our seats at the officials' desk, where she speaks of adjusting to her first year responsibilities as head trainer and dealing with a promising team like this one. She seems to focus upon the six sophomores who as seniors in high school were each rated as bluechips, national top ten recruits. They are the ones who pose the greatest challenge. Roxann speaks of the difficulty she has responding not to the physiologies of these women but to their psyches. She explains that when players enter the training room en masse, she readies and dispenses with treatment according to the nature of their injuries. But the players expect treatment according to different, shifting criteria: who came in first, who is more cooperative, who is this or that. She admits that she's still getting used to the players, that they don't quite understand her yet. The assessment of pain seems a constant struggle for Roxann. How much pain is too much? For the answer, she accords players considerable authority in determining when and how long they play. And yet, because players often underestimate pain in their desire to play, Roxann remains the responsive but final arbiter.

I realize that in this context of learning one's injury has repercussions for her teammates. The tragedy of yesterday, Simone's fateful surgery and its subsequent diagnosis, has already begun to affect players and trainers. Roxann seems defensive. Malikah's brusque appeals for an MRI have had a delayed effect, and I listen to Roxann speak to me of her frustration with Malikah, who since July and August has grown "non-compliant" in her rehab.

The coaches enter the arena at a quick pace, strolling toward center court as Coach Lee calls the team to stretch. Players find a patch of hardwood around the center circle and begin stretching to the instructions of the player assigned to lead. Meanwhile, Coach Lee speaks to the group, soliciting ideas for educational programs the men's and women's athletic departments are currently organizing for student athletes. Jenny suggests a panel on "Proper Undergarments for Street Clothing." Her teammates offer other equally creative suggestions. Humor seems a way for the players to manage the endless obligations they are asked to meet. In addition to academic and athletic responsibilities, the team visits pediatric wards, reads in local elementary schools, attends autograph signings, hosts senior high school recruits, and responds to hundreds of letters from fans.

Roxann returns to the officials' desk at midcourt where I commonly sit during practices. It is 6:15 AM. The players have just entered into a weave drill desperately short of players. Tiffany's knees keep her courtside, where she begins her rehab. Angie's neuralgic ankle sprain commits her to a morning of whirlpool, exercise bike, and ice. Substitute players today, managers Jeremy and Michael join the squad. On the perimeter, the young men are masters of the hand-check. Inside, when they find themselves suddenly caught at a height disadvantage, they make up for lost inches, applying their upper bodies against the backs of centers with unrelenting pressure. The centers must bear this weight as they position and reposition themselves in the lane. Substituting for players when they are injured or absent, both Jeremy and Michael know the offensive and defensive configurations so well that on a given day, they can actualize the role of any absent player.

On this day, Michael's first shot is thrown up uncharacteristically hard, bouncing off the backboard well beyond net. Coach Lee, standing near the officials' desk, turns to Roxann and me with a smile, "Boy, he's lucky he's not a girl. I would have chewed him out for that one." With that, Coach Lee spots Tiffany, who jumps rope on the sidelines, "Tiffany, would you get rid of that junior high jump rope stuff? You're double jumping!"

During the next half-hour, from 6:30 to 7:00 AM, the intensity of play nosedives. Players run more slowly, pivoting with less exactness, and passing with less snap of the wrist. At one point, watching a shooting drill, Coach Lee explodes, "God dang it! You three down there follow your shot! Follow your shot!" Minutes later, I turn to a portion of the floor in which Coach Peeples leads a drill. I catch her sharp words to Malikah, "I'm not putting up with that. Jeremy, come here." Jeremy takes Malikah's place on the court. Hearing Coach Peeples, Coach Lee strolls toward Malikah, who is wandering off the court. I hear Coach Lee speak to Malikah in a firm, serious tone. A minute later Malikah heads to the nearest arena stairway, which she begins ascending at a jog. For five minutes, she will jog up and down the steps until Coach Lee calls her back. Malikah does not rejoin Coach Peeples's group. She goes where Coach Lee places her, where she will stay the remainder of the drill.

At 7:00 AM, the sun has yet to rise, and I begin to feel as if I'm trapped in a subterranean vault. Sunlight has yet to radiate through windows that circle the upper concourse. When it does, for a fifteen-minute stretch, windows facing the east will admit light that beams to the cellar of the arena, where players, coaches, and managers will be temporarily blinded at particular points on the floor. But all that is still forty minutes away.

At 7:12 AM, Coach Lee calls together two groups, guards and posts who have been working at separate baskets. She announces that given the confusion about the 2–3 zone, she has decided to make an adjustment. She alludes to the problematic wing position, where high and low players always experience a moment of confusion. When does the forward assume responsibility for defending the wing? When does the point guard relinquish responsibility? These have been the questions. Coach Lee decrees, "I want baseline forwards to play it until the guard gets you off." The announcement places pressure on players who must now recalibrate their bodies and perception.

After initial practice in the 2–3 zone, Coach Lee initiates a half-court scrimmage. She announces that turnovers for either side will connote sprints for all. With each turnover, play ceases and players head to the nearest baseline where they initiate a full-court, round-trip sprint. In the midst of a scrimmage segment, Jenny receives a pass and begins a topside post-maneuver that she bungles when she brings the ball down into a defensive player's slashing hands. She jams her finger and releases the ball. Another turnover. Players return to the baseline, one of them asking, "Jenny, you alright?" Jenny begins the sprint, remarking tersely, "No, I'm not."

Ten minutes into the drill, in yet another segment of scrimmage, players are visibly tired. Karen advances the ball slowly, and her teammates downcourt take advantage of time, leaning over, grabbing the hems of their shorts, breathing hard. They resist movement, but Coach Lee is insistent. Spotting Tangela harboring in the paint, she announces, "You only got three seconds in there. Don't be campin'!"

Finally, Coach Lee calls a timeout, "Twenty second timeout. Twenty second timeout. Get a drink. Hurry."

The players drink, cough, spit, breathe deeply, and return. No time to sit and when Coach Lee sees players leaning, she remarks, "Nobody grab your knees. You're not tired. It's the last four minutes of the game."

It is now 7:45 AM, and sunlight penetrates the arena. Coach Lee announces the final drill, "Simone's last request was Jamaican Lay-ups." Simone, a native of Jamaica, had coined the drill and now, a year later, is again its object. The announcement has a deathly nuance to it. The players are quiet, taking extra moments to recall a drill they have not performed this season. Initiating play, they stop and start, lining up wrong on baselines and misfiring passes. Coach Lee appeals to the group, "Communication is your best way to figure something out!" Turning her back to the court and walking toward me at the officials' desk, Lee places the burden of perceptual responsibility on her players, who continue to bumble their way through the drill. Tiffany, who some time ago finished her extended warm-up and joined the team, now stops the group, holding the ball while she attempts to explain the drill. Nadine remarks from twenty feet away, "No, no, no."

Tiffany reasserts herself, "We know it, ladies. Let's just do this!"

The confusion continues. Coach Lee turns and watches, "Figure it out." I wait for her voice to explode, but she is patient, standing staunchly with arms folded.

Finally, the players slip into sync, running and shooting with uninterrupted fluidity. Coach Lee speaks again, this time insistent and even-toned, "Do this because Simone can't. Feel fortunate you're able to do this. She'd give anything for the pain you're feeling now. Go hard."

Go hard." Minutes later, Coach Lee has isolated Jenny for attention, "Jenny, you're very close to starting this five minutes over. Get your arms moving!" To the managers who are timing the drill, Coach Lee orders, "From this three minutes forward, let me know who misses." Spotting Jenny, she remarks again, "That's better, Jenny. Come on." And to Nadine, "That's the one you're missing in a game, Nadine. That's the one you gotta be strong on!"

With less than two minutes remaining in the full-court lay-up drill, Coach Myers yells, "Way to get stronger, Hawks!" Coach Lee follows, "I'm going to keep bringing it up. It's a minute and a half that you have that Simone doesn't have." Again, I feel that someone has died. Nadine runs and counts down the clock, "Thirty seconds, ladies. Thirty seconds!" Soon, she reports again, "Fifteen seconds, ladies. Fifteen seconds!" Somewhere, Nadine finds the strength to run, breathe, and talk. Only Malikah joins her in the endeavor, "Come on, ladies." The other players concentrate on two basic tasks, running hard and shooting to make.

The minutes end, and players gear down their sprints to an even walk that leads them toward Coach Lee at center court. They have endured a practice without injury. Players walk to the circle with their hands on hips. Their breathing is deep, punctuated by coughs. Coach Lee interrupts, "Good job, ladies. Keep walking. Communicate and help each other and you can do anything! We had one lapse on the defensive drill. We'll make it up tomorrow. You've got weights today. Who's got tests and papers?" Shannon raises her hand and announces an impending paper. Nadine notes an exam in her Judeo-Christian Traditions course. Jenny groans, acknowledging her need to complete and submit an art portfolio. Soon, the team huddles. Coach Lee forms the core of the huddle, extending her hand so that others can add theirs to an ascending pile of down-turned palms. The huddle is tight with each concentric circle of players leaning lightly upon the backs and shoulders of those inside. Roxann, Doug, and the four managers move toward the huddle. Unable to reach the inner circle, they seem content to grab the backs of t-shirts belonging to posts who form the outer sphere. The assistant coaches are melded into various rings of what is now a tight-pressed cluster of sweating bodies.

I spot Tangela's trademark red bandana on the far side of the huddle, but her head is bent toward the circle, so that is all I see. With hands together atop Coach Lee's, and on count of four, the circle moves and speaks as one, arms rising and falling, bodies pressing and releasing, to a chorused "Team Unity!" The group seems to hold together a few extra seconds this morning, but gradually outer rings give way and players disassemble, some advancing to the baseline for water, others conferring with coaches or walking to the weight room. I notice that before Tangela leaves the floor, Coach Lee pulls her aside. I hear the word "Simone" and know that for a long time this word will carry great weight.

Later, I would speak to several players about Coach Lee's desire to intensify Simone's image at the close of practice. Was Coach Lee using Simone's individual pain for collective gain in a way they resented? Both Jenny and Tangela were adamant. The request "Do it because Simone can't" had been a way of remembering Simone, of connecting her name to their own potentiality. For Jenny and Tangela, absence had become presence in the motion and mindset Simone's drill required.

I decide to forego the weight room today. Shannon has asked to speak with me at breakfast about two Paule Marshall books, *Brown Girl, Brownstones* and *Praisesong for the Widow*. Both form the basis of her paper for Literature of African Peoples. Leaving the arena, I pass through the tunnel to the hospitality room, where Jim, training table chef to both male and female athletes, scrambles dozens of eggs in a large skillet. His movement is restricted to a small portion of the room, a kitchen area that includes less than ten feet of counter space, two refrigerators, and two stoves, cramped quarters for a man who prepares morning training tables, pregame meals, and various other special functions for players, journalists, and athletic personnel. Sitting at one of four banquet tables, I begin a hasty review of my own copies of Marshall's books. My preparation will be inadequate, but at least this stretch of thirty minutes, while the players lift weights, will afford me time to collect my thoughts.

At 8:35 AM, Coach Myers enters the hospitality room, greeting Jim with a warm hello and the inquiry, "What do we have this morning, Jim?" She is delighted to learn that biscuits and gravy are on the menu. Jim smiles, wipes his hands across his white apron, and announces that the buffet is ready. To players and coaches, Jim is irreplaceable. The risk, perhaps, is that he seems permanent. In fact, he has grown weary of athletic administrators who in his mind seem little concerned with the procedural details that he takes seriously. Lifting a Styrofoam plate from the stack at the start of the buffet line, I follow on Coach Myers's heels, dipping into a series of elegant chafing dishes and leaving spilled food that Jim quietly swipes away. Coach Lee follows, and the three of us sink into folding chairs at one of four banquet tables. When both coaches have finished with condiments that rest in the middle of the table, I layer my hash browns with catsup and my pancakes with maple syrup. Coach Lee surveys her own plate, turns to me, and smiles, "So, Julie, no secrets here. What are you seeing and thinking?"

Both coaches wait for a response. Again, I politely repeat the rather vague spiel that I am looking for the features that define players' athletic learning. I talk about my interest in the conceptual significance of the human body. Coaches Henrickson and Peeples join us, and the conversation turns to daily schedules. I note my astonishment at their long days.

"Well, you should see us in the afternoons when we get together," Coach Lee remarks. "By then, we don't even know what we're saying to one another."

"The other night," Coach Lee continues, "Bonnie and I were reviewing game tape at my place. At around 10:00 I asked her, 'What about practice tomorrow?' And then I fell asleep. When I woke up, she was gone."

At 8:45 AM players file in at a staggered pace. They are showered and dressed for the day. The early birds are the healthiest, for they require little or no postgame treatment. Tangela fills her plate and sits next to me. Shannon enters and returns Tangela's "Waiting to Exhale" CD that she has used to dub her own copy. Coach Lee asks for clarification from anyone who will answer, "Is that the CD to the Whitney Houston movie?"

She receives a collective affirmation from players, just what she needs to stand and deliver an uproarious Bobby Brown rampage. Nadine comes to Bobby's immediate defense and the defense of "dirty dogs" everywhere. She begins humming his notorious "Humpin' Around." Preparing to sit, Angie decides against the chair next to Nadine, whose body sings and moves with such enthusiasm that space around her evaporates. Angie selects a chair across the table from Nadine.

"How do you put up with your roommate," I call out to Angie with a smile.

"I don't know," she says. "I guess Nay is my cross to bear."

Nadine ceases her rendition of "Humpin' Around" and announces, once again, her Judeo final. She wears gray sweats and a dark-shaded camouflage hunting cap, bill to the back. The determinism versus free will debate vis-a-vis women's relationships with men continues, a surviving thread of the earlier Whitney Houston–Bobby Brown theme. Shannon remarks, "Hurt me once, shame on you. Hurt me twice, shame on me."

"Oh, I usually give 'em three," Coach Myers remarks.

"You just get hurt, pick up the pieces, and go on about your business," Nadine says with a shrug.

Angie, Shannon, and Tangela argue halfheartedly with Nadine, realizing within moments their words fall short of effect.

"Nay, you crazy!" Tangela says finally. And then, turning to me, remarks, "What do you call somebody who causes trouble?"

Slow to words, I tell her I can't think. Tangela turns and repeats the question to Coach Myers who suggests, "an antagonist." Sitting back from her plate, Tangela turns to Nadine, who is on her left, and replies straight-faced, "You're an antagonist." Suddenly, Nadine sits up straight in her chair and feigns astonishment.

Tangela grows quiet as she rolls the base of her right foot on a bag of ice. The plantar fasciaitis again. I tap her knee and tell her she did a good job in practice. Then I return to the buffet line, where Jim serves me another waffle. Rather than return to my seat, I join Shannon. We begin discussing *Brown Girl, Brownstones* as talk swirls around us. Soon the room has cleared of coaches and players and a second shift of athletic facilities workers has arrived. After that will come a third shift, women's athletic support staff. For now, though, the focus is a discussion of the character Selena. Periodically, Jim passes by the table to pour Shannon hot tea, which soothes her swollen throat. Though she must swallow hard to talk, Shannon is animated in her references to Selena.

We turn to Avey, the central character in Marshall's *Praisesong for the Widow*, a character who puzzles Shannon. I feel strange becoming Avey's advocate. We are different in more ways than we are alike to be sure, but I connect with her fear of transition. In the midst of a doctoral program that has come to seem eternal, I find it hard to envision my own future. But all that seems beyond Shannon, who admits she is impatient with Avey's hesitance.

At 10:30 AM Shannon and I finish our conversation. She has enough to begin writing. And I have enough to know that Shannon's sense of competition clearly extends to her academic work, as I have heard during our hour of discussion frequent references to grades. Shannon accepts my offer of a ride to Student Health, where she plans to see a doctor about her cold. I apologize for my compact car beforehand, which offers little accommodation to players and their gear. Shannon doesn't seem to mind, talking instead about her plan to study in the dorm before taking two exams later in the day. She yearns for tomorrow, her first occasion in days to "really sleep." As I watch Shannon lift her book-laden gym bag and depart toward the clinic, I wonder not only where she gets her energy and stamina but, more generally, what sustains her.

Success: The Interdependence of Mind and Body in Activity

In varying degrees across the tenures of Stringer and Lee, biographical associations contributed to a system of apprenticeship that accorded coaches and elder players considerable responsibility for the teaching of positional knowledge and the sharing of ritual and memory. While novices had opportunities to invent and intensify rituals, their primary responsibility was to learn the bodily activity that insured relational knowing.

Entering into a collective perceptual field is an inherently political process. For young players to submit to acculturation, care from master players and coaches is requisite. As Nadine explained,

> Well, you stay with these people. You eat, sleep, wake up with them. Every time you turn around there's one of your teammates next to you, or behind you, or in front of you. It becomes a sense of bonding. Once you sign that paper you're bonded to the women's basketball team. There's a community. I thank God for my team. I thank God for sending me here because I continue to grow. There are a lot more sisters on the team. I put myself in positions, or I find myself in positions, where I see my sisters, either African American or white. I got somebody to comfort. I got comfort.

In *The Last Shot: City Streets, Basketball Dreams*, essayist Darcy Frey writes that "sports psychologists and guidance counselors . . . often talk about an essential triangle in a player's life formed by his family, his neighborhood, and his schooling. The rule is that a player can triumph over one weak point in that triangle, maybe two, but almost never three" (1994, 186). For the Hawkeye women, who live apart from their families and neighborhoods, the essential triangle consists of coaches, teammates, and support staff. These relationships altered during liminal periods when the sudden absence of a coach or player disrupted relational knowing.

On the morning of Simone's absence, anti-structure did not appear to be a collective experience. Malikah's hesitation seemed markedly greater than her teammates'. Fearful of what Simone's injury might suggest about her own, Malikah's search for meaning was, understandably, less participatory than self-oriented. Because players had responded in varying degrees, Coach Lee's decision to end practice with the Jamaican Lay-up Drill seemed an act of ritual intensification that reminded players of their commitment both to Simone and to the sustenance of the team.

From the time of Simone's injury to mid-December, the Hawkeye women ascend the national rankings. By the arrival of the Carolina Holiday Beach Classic, they are ranked #11 in the Associated Press poll with a 6–0 mark. Simone's absence has demanded reintegration among coaches and players, leaving Karen to guide a team laden with sophomores. She does so with quiet resolve, and team "chemistry" is apparent for the first time in eighteen months. While the Hawkeyes lose to #10 Georgia in the North Carolina tournament, they return to Iowa City with impressive nonconference victories against #13 Kansas and #16 North Carolina. Across their three nonconference tournaments, Nadine, Tangela, Karen, and Tiffany have received most valuable player and all-tournament team awards. The absence of a single scoring leader suggests the Hawkeye women are achieving systemic balance.

Notes

1. During 1981–1982, a series of ritual and theatre conferences stimulated interdisciplinary interest in the concept of performance. Key foci included performance as a transformative phenomenon, genres and stages of performance, the concept of sociodrama, the transmission of performance knowledge, and the relation of performer and audience. Soon after these conferences, the deaths of key participants Erving Goffman, Barbara Myerhoff, and Victor Turner led to organized interest in performance studies. Richard Schechner would become an important figure, authoring key texts and using his editorship of *TDR* to sustain cross-disciplinary investigations of performance.

2. Drawing from the work of van Gennep (1960), Victor Turner (1969) explored liminality as the performative flux located between structure and antistructure. He considered liminality a feature of both individual and social activity. Liminality is a necessarily reflexive experience that moves an individual or group to understand through the condition of an other. Carpsecken (1993) emphasizes that liminality is the "well-spring for acts of creativity and resistance" (278). For analyses of liminality see McLaren (1993) and Myerhoff (1975, 1978).

Chapter Three

The Efficacy of Emotion

After you've been playing with the same people for a while, you almost start to get on the same brain waves. . . . They understand what I'm thinking, and I understand what they're thinking. It's comfortable. I think that's what makes a team successful. If you know that person is going to be there without even having to look at them, you can always depend on them being there.

Jenny Noll

Once the players have mastered the system, a powerful group intelligence emerges that is greater than the coach's ideas or those of any individual on the team.

Phil Jackson and Hugh Delehanty,
Sacred Hoops (1995)

During the early months of the 1995–1996 season, relational knowing does not come easily for the Hawkeyes. While successive nonconference wins suggest players' conceptual understanding has cohered, fits and starts arise. Nadine, in particular, seems to struggle. With Karen and Stacy, a freshman reserve, slotted at point guard, Nadine continues to learn the positional knowledge required of her shift this season to the wing, where offensive objectives suddenly include three-point scoring, increased ball rotation to the lane, and new vectors of body movement. On defense, Nadine must acclimate to the activity required of zone and player-on-player formations and weak side defensive assignments. On occasion, Nadine compensates for her confusion with street moves that do not coincide with what coaches and teammates expect from her position. When it occurs, her eruptive play earns a standard redress from Coach Lee, "Nadine, I don't think there's a day that goes by that you don't try to do things all by yourself." No option exists for Nadine but to learn offensive and defensive assignments, a process that will require enormous physical and conceptual sacrifice. To some extent, she must unlearn her history as point guard.

In late January, the Hawkeye women travel to Northwestern University for a Sunday afternoon match-up. Games in Evanston are never easy, but this trip will be particularly troublesome. The Wildcats are ranked #17 in the AP poll and threaten the Iowa women with a balanced shooting attack. On game day Welsh-Ryan Arena fills with more road-tripping Iowans than locals, proof that the Hawkeyes' accelerated race toward the Big Ten title has renewed fan support. Following an intense game and victory, the Iowa women are euphoric. Supporters in attendance continue celebrating well after the Wildcats have surrendered their floor, and a sportscaster taping postgame commentary for an eastern Iowa television station captures the sentiments of players immediately after the game. Relinquishing his microphone, the reporter remains out of view as players respond impromptu before the camera. The footage will appear the next evening in segments broadcast at 5:20, 6:20, and 10:20 PM. Each report begins with Tangela, who comments on the victory before passing the microphone to "my girl, Nadine."

With a shift of the lens, Malikah and Nadine enter the frame. Nadine's left hand grips the microphone as she slips into dialect to recount her own pregame saga, a loss of footwear that resulted in her entire game in a pair of borrowed, grossly-oversized Reeboks. The verbal play is Nadine "unplugged." Looking on in surprise, Malikah offers only silence when Nadine finally aims the microphone in her direction. To me, an evening later, the segment is delightful. I enjoy Nadine's spirit, realizing just how much the Northwestern victory has hinged upon her acculturation to a new position. I give no thought to the fact that she is appearing before a public who will understand her dialect and animation less in terms of its wit than its "appropriateness."

The next Tuesday morning, excitement is palpable among the players as they prepare for practice. They report to each other on weekend upsets among the top AP poll spots. The Hawkeyes continue to ascend, this week rising to #8 in the national poll. As team members stretch at center court, Coach Lee enters into an unusually formal register.

"As you're stretching, I want to say that I think we've reached a critical point that's worth discussing. Up to this point it's been a team effort. Each and every game someone's stepped up. That's what makes you great."

I try to anticipate where Lee is heading, particularly as she has rarely accorded past victories and greatness much attention.

"You've begun to make true believers of everyone. But if you start to believe the hype, you'll be in trouble."

As she speaks, Coach Lee roams the circle of players with her arms crossed tightly in front of her. Periodically, she stops to make eye contact with players who, lying on their backs, have no alternative but to look back. In a sudden transition, Lee shifts to the Channel 2 sports segment. She praises Tangela for her poise before shifting in exasperation to Nadine.

"Nadine, if someone puts a mike in front of your face, you better know what to do with it."

Nadine continues stretching. Across the circle, Coach Lee extols the importance of "control."

"Malikah," she adds, "you were right to stand back and watch Nadine."

As Nadine falls under fire, I feel guilty, an accomplice who just minutes before practice had shared my positive reaction. Now, I listen to Coach Lee as if she is talking to me directly. Broadcast to the regional public, the segment has reached the eyes and ears of predominantly white viewers, who by and large will have responded with confusion, perhaps even disapproval. Despite a top-ten ranking, Coach Lee can not afford to alienate fans. Implicitly, her message is clear. Successful athletic programs earn and maintain their fans through behavior that affirms the conventions of the status quo. By the coach's decree, the dialect and body language are limited to team members only.

Coach Lee's response emanates from her own embodied location in an institutional hierarchy dependent on the material support of the public. While Lee's own gregarious nature inclines her to acts of unleashed spontaneity during practices, she exhibits restraint in public appearances. From her players, she expects the same adjustments. Drawing attention to Nadine, Coach Lee seems both to instruct and to discipline. Concerning the latter, cultural critic John Fiske (1993) has noted that

> Discipline always carries the apparently contradictory forces of submission and empowerment. A disciplined person is one who submits him- or herself to the power of a particular way of knowing/behaving in order to participate in that power, to become more effective in applying it and thus to gain the satisfaction and rewards that it offers. (64)

Unlike many head coaches who forbid younger student athletes from media contact, Lee enacts no such restrictions. Still, the creation of public personae is significant enough to be represented among the team's five goals for this season, "Know what you say and how you say it." The bottom line for players and coaches is that media representatives attend to those who reliably fulfill the performative expectations of the general public. For players who value visibility, media performances are centrally important. Straight commentary not creativity is the rule.

In the media opportunities that follow, Nadine assumes a stoical stance, providing just the facts to sportscasters who insert her cleanly into postgame footage. Within the institutional framework that has led to her discipline, Nadine grows more powerful. I wonder, though, to what extent this power whitens her world in ways that jeopardize her embodied history. Signithia Fordham (1993) suggests that "gender diversity" is difficult for women of color to maintain,

> . . . like most other women of color, African-American women are compelled to consume the universalized images of white American women, including body image, linguistic patterns, styles of interacting, and so forth. Because womanhood or femaleness is norm referenced to one group—white middle-class Americans—women from social groups who do not share this racial, ethnic, or cultural legacy are compelled to silence or gender 'passing.' (8)

Restricting aspects of her bodily knowledge to the backstage, I wonder what it means that Nadine has been asked to reorient her identity in light of the desires of a predominantly white audience. Two years later, when I share this textualized moment with Nadine, she will express displeasure at my inscription, underscoring her belief that Coach Lee had responded appropriately. She wants readers to understand that the moment fostered her development as a team leader, "When I do go into the real world, it's not going to be all African American. . . . Most of the time it's predominantly white. So I have to learn to deal with something outside of what I'm used to."

Though Nadine and I considered the moment important to self-definition, we varied in our understanding of its qualitative effect. I continue to wonder if we might both be right. Politically speaking, performative adjustments on and off the court heightened Nadine's status as a player, particularly during her junior year when yet another shift, a return to point guard, would earn her increased media attention. In Nadine's mind, the act of volitional subordination in this instance served her broader objectives, which included acclimation to a predominantly white public. For Nadine, adjustments in verbal and bodily activity that Lee advocated were a means of consolidating power. From my location, inarguably one of racial and class privilege, subordination seemed as much about loss as gain. Aspects of racial and gender difference were dimensions of the body that players rarely volunteered to discuss. Only in private conversations did I learn that some student athletes worried about the dissolution of difference. During her long recuperation, Simone and I had talked about her ongoing struggle to sustain her own identity in the context of team rituals that necessitated a relational way of knowing on and off the court. Bearing long dreadlocks, a Jamaican accent, and a powerful stature, Simone remarked to me, "I'm Jamaican. I talk different. I look different. I'm just different." The danger for a team is that the bodily activity that fosters a reflexive consciousness becomes counterproductive when it threatens to erase players' embodied histories, histories carved by difference. The perpetual dilemma for players and coaches is to recognize and sustain identities of difference in the midst of public pressures to be the same and conceptual pressures to think the same.

Things Fall Apart

Every time a basketball player takes a step, an entire new geometry of action is created around [her]. In ten seconds, with or without the ball, a good player may see perhaps a hundred alternatives and, from them, make half a dozen choices as [she] goes along. A great player will see even more alternatives and will make more choices, and this multiradial way of looking at things can carry over into [her] life.

Bill Bradley, qtd. in *A Sense of Where You Are* (McPhee 1999)

Though injuries, position reassignments, and illness have influenced learning during the nonconference season, practices rarely pass without moments of contagious improvisational humor. Nadine and Jenny take full advantage of the opportunities Coach Lee allows for comic relief, and those players like Tangela, who often appear weighted by the level of expectation fans reserve for them, relax. In mid-December during a practice when players seem generally tired and low, Coach Lee suddenly interrupts a drill in progress to initiate a game of half-court freeze tag. She announces that coaches, too, will play, that—in fact—they are "it." Assistants Myers and Peeples seem startled at the announcement but soon join in, working together to corral and tag players. Noise erupts as taller players succumb first to coaches. In the midst of immobilizing a player by touch, Coach Lee chastises Tiffany who leaps to life before her actual liberation. Tiffany jests, "You have to explain the rules prior to the start of play!" In just minutes, the players seem invigorated. From the frivolity of freeze tag, Coach Lee calls the players to the baseline for Olympic Shooting, a six-minute drill for which they will set a field goal record that stands the season.

In early February, the Hawkeyes rise to #6 in the AP poll before entering a series of conference games against ranked opponents. In mid-February, the team begins the final stretch of the 1995–1996 season undefeated in Big Ten play. Having weathered preseason and early conference games, intercollegiate student athletes often begin to wear down at this point in the season. Regardless of its win or loss record, a team can enter into the February Funk, a period when players are often courted by complacency and lose sight of objectives that may have guided their individual and collective play all season.

During a practice on February 8, the day before a weekend road trip to Michigan State and Purdue, Coach Lee is frank with players, "Ladies, I'm not sleeping well. We're not playing good post defense. We're too content to allow ourselves to get pinned."

On the Saturday between a Michigan State win and the Purdue contest, I visit the University Inn in West Lafayette, where the team harbors before its pivotal Sunday contest with the Purdue Boilermakers. Though I am staying with local friends during my visit, I have arranged to tutor players during this off day. Set apart from the university and the city of West Lafayette, the hotel occupies a lonely plot of land, fringed only by a distant Wal-Mart and fast food restaurant. The dank interior of its lobby leaves me uncomfortable, and I'm glad to spot Nadine and Tangela soon after I enter. Nadine offers me a handshake before Tangela escorts me to the remaining players. We pass the front desk, and I wave at Shannon Perry, who sits in the manager's office typing a paper for her Interpretation of Literature class.

Tangela leads me to a first floor hallway filled with Hawkeye players in every manner of contortion. In their black and gold nylon sweatsuits, they use the corridor to talk and stretch, attempts to battle both boredom and exhaustion. Following a win at Michigan State last night, players, coaches, and managers braved blizzard conditions aboard a bus that eventually arrived in West Lafayette. Now, they are only just waking after fitful sleeps punctuated by muscle cramping. Confined in bus seats for hours, players' bodies pay a price today. The malaise is palpable.

On Sunday afternoon, Mackey Arena will do little to counter players' stagnation of spirit. The secret to winning in this arena depends upon several factors. First, visiting teams must adjust to its subterranean bench seats, which frustrate a coach's ability to see the floor and to communicate with players. Second, visiting teams must calibrate their shots to the metal rims of both hoops, which are notoriously hard and often prompt players not simply to soften shots but to soften approaches to the basket, a deadly compensatory response. Third, Mackey Arena is a site of iconic overkill. Boilermaker Pete, a hypermasculine buffoon in muscle and hard hat, is joined at halftime by the strutting Golden Girl and her back-up Silver Twins, female dancers clad in one-piece metallic swimsuits who stir the home crowd in a seamy sideshow.

The disruptive influence of architecture and iconography will not be the only problems in this game. In January, during the first of two meetings, the Hawkeyes had used their defensive press to rattle the Boilermakers in Carver-Hawkeye Arena, prompting a come-from-behind victory that had left gregarious Purdue coach Linn Dunn uncharacteristically subdued. During that game, Tangela had poured in a career high 27 points and 13 rebounds; Tiffany Gooden had defied pain to supply 14 points of her own, and Stacy had stepped off the bench for a series of crucial free throws. The loss had been embarrassing to upperclass Purdue players, who would certainly vow a different outcome in this second game of the conference season.

From the tipoff, the Hawkeyes' play at Purdue is nightmarish. Iowa fans wait for a player, any player, to take initiative, but it seems the players themselves are waiting. Under the leadership of freshman point guard Stephanie White, the Purdue starters and reserves orchestrate a tenacious defense, immobilizing the Hawkeye women throughout the first half. Few anticipate that White and teammate Ukari Figgs will lead the Boilermakers to a national championship title in three years and that they will pass through three head coaches en route. For now, the Boilermakers attune themselves to the moment. Inside the lane, they collapse upon Tangela, who is pinned on the blocks by defenders who double-team her on the high and low sides. In the stands, I sit behind Tangela's family, who has traveled from Chicago. Stephanie, her mother, sits stiff and silent on the bleachers. Though I sense the onset of fear in Tangela's play and demeanor, I do not require confirmation. Stephanie's bearing reflects her worry. By late in the first half, the Purdue lead extends to double digits. During time-outs, Iowa players listen to coaches as if in isolation, hardly acknowledging their connections to each other. When play resumes, reserves who have relinquished their seats return to a passive sideline vigil, rarely warning teammates on court about screens and backdoor cuts. Not a single Iowa player or reserve escapes paralysis, and the Hawkeye women leave Mackey with their first conference defeat, an ugly twenty-point loss that SportsChannel has televised to the nation.

At 5:55 AM the next Tuesday morning, coaches and players gather in the women's basketball lounge for the first practice since the defeat. While players are expected to review game tape on their own time, sessions like this one allow Lee the chance to isolate key episodes for study. Players are aware that the team has fallen to #7 in the AP poll released Monday. Today they are somber. When Lee enters the team lounge, she takes a position before the expansive glass case of conference and tournament trophies. She is stern but patient as Rani, a senior manager, fidgets with the remote control to a videocassette recorder that feeds a large-screen television. Players and coaches wait in awkward silence as Rani scrutinizes the game tape at fast forward. She struggles to locate the start of the second half, and Shannon attempts to help, "No, that's still the first half." Finally, Coach Lee interrupts, "That's good. We'll just start there." Lee accepts the remote control from Rani and turns to the players, "I want you to watch this film and tell me what it reminds you of."

With that, she pushes the play button. In less than a minute, Jenny remarks, "A lot of games."

"That's right, Jenny. A *lot* of games." Coach Lee speaks to the history of this team, to its slow starts and unpredictable cold spells. The University of Georgia, the team's single nonconference loss this season, and now the Purdue debacle make clear the vulnerability that will only become more consequential as the season continues. This year, both at home and away, the Iowa women have rarely established a commanding presence in the early minutes of games. Success has depended on one or two players, different each game, to establish leadership. Tangela, a leading point scorer and rebounder, experiences acute apprehension at the start of games and rarely warms up before the middle of the first period.

Coach Lee scans the players, who face her in two tiers of gray couches with mauve trim, "If you can't take criticism today, you better leave. Each and every one of you is going to receive it."

Restarting the game tape, Lee begins a terse commentary. Sitting farthest from the television monitor, Tiffany rests her head in both hands, glancing at the television from a sideways angle. Jenny slumps in the second row. I stand behind and to the side of the couches, where I can watch players' responses without intruding. Each pause, rewind, and play sequence prolongs the agony of an outcome that is already known. Midway through the tape, Stacy shifts from the back row to the carpet, where she stretches out stomach first. Karen moves as well. Despite the movement, players remain attentive and silent, heeding Coach Lee, who highlights lapses in individual technique and team play. Pausing and rewinding the tape, Lee identifies problems and recommends adjustments. As the tape reveals the final minutes of the game, Coach Lee points at the screen, "Look at that," she groans. "Look at that."

I look. What I see is an aggressive Purdue team huddled at the key during a momentary break in action. They form a tight circle. A few feet away, Iowa players wander lost in their own orbits. The images speak for themselves. As the game tape ends, players know without command to proceed to the parquet. In the walk to the tunnel, Coach Lee greets me.

"Good morning, Julie. Well, did we fall apart or what?"

Like her assistants, Lee wears a t-shirt today emblazoned on its front with the words "Never Fear. Never Quit" in bold, black letters. A bald eagle, talons spread for prey, consumes the back of each shirt. The motto says much about how these coaches understand themselves and their jobs. Except for Coach Myers, an assistant with Lee during the Stringer years, coaches Henrickson and Peeples are new hires who share scouting and recruiting responsibilities. Together, the group of four work in ways that seem at times collaborative and at times competitive. Without exception, they demand no more from players than they demand of themselves. Like the players, their work begins at 5:30 AM with practice and continues well into the evening when each coach studies opponents' game tapes. From this analysis, each produces the written scouting reports central to players' preparation.

This morning, as Coach Lee and I walk through the tunnel, she admits the Purdue loss is a blessing, a source of motivation unlike those that eliminate possibilities in tournament play. As she meditates upon the loss, I realize there is something symbolic about this moment of transit. From the team lounge, where players and coaches negotiate and affirm their intentions, the tunnel is a portal to play. In its concrete and conceptual effect, the tunnel directs players and coaches from past to present, from private to public, from objective to outcome. Each practice and game, the recurring ritual of procession allows a team the opportunity to begin anew or, at the least, to begin again.

As we enter the arena proper, Coach Lee walks to the center circle where players stretch.

"Know this," she announces, "we coaches love each and every one of you. Put the past behind you. We're going to win the Big Ten."

Games across the Big Ten during the coming weekend will likely determine the conference champion. It is already Tuesday. Friday evening the Hawkeyes host the 9th-ranked Penn State Nittany Lions, reigning and contending Big Ten champions. On Saturday, the team will travel by bus to Madison, Wisconsin, for a Sunday contest against the 11th-ranked Wisconsin Badgers. The next two games will demand more from players than any stretch of play this season.

Wednesday morning I enter Carver-Hawkeye to find players hastily assembling in the training room. They are behind schedule and know it. I learn that the freshman manager responsible for transporting players from Slater Dormitory has overslept for the fourth time this season. As I enter the arena, I move to a theater seat on the perimeter, steering clear of Rani, who is furious. Like the players, managers learn by apprenticeship. After four mishaps, Rani is no longer willing to assume responsibility for lapses in the performance of this novice. Set apart from all this, Karen occupies a fetal position at the base of a main basket. She is in the midst of a break-up with a boyfriend who has struggled all season to accommodate her commitment to sport. Malikah sits a few feet away from Karen donning headphones connected to a CD player. She waves to me before turning her gaze to the far end of the floor, an empty space that harbors no one. For several days, Malikah's headphones have seemed a means of detachment from those in her midst. I know that she remains afraid of injury, that she thinks often of her infant stepbrother at home with her mother in Cleveland, and that she wishes for more from basketball. Other players seem distracted as well. Tangela has convinced herself she is in a slump. And Angie Hamblin, still struggling with her ankle injury, worries about her father's worsening heart condition.

Coach Lee enters the arena in silence. She spots the young manager, who sits alone at a distant temporary basket. Lee approaches the manager, and though her words are inaudible, the young woman's deepening slump hardly requires one to guess. On several occasions I have heard Coach Lee speak warily of the manager's tardiness to Coach Myers, who oversees support personnel. After several minutes, Lee rises and walks to center court. The manager, shedding tears, departs the arena. She has lost her job and will not return. Such is the level of expectation coaches, players, and managers reserve for each other.

Before joining her teammates at the center circle, Susan asks if we can reschedule a tutoring appointment. I admit that I, too, am behind. Reassuring me that she has started Chinua Achebe's *Things Fall Apart*, she hurries to center court, promising to have the book finished when we meet. I admire her stamina. She struggles to shake perpetual bronchitis, to earn a starting position at the wing, and to complete the requirements for a major and teaching certificate in history. I think ahead to the spring semester of her senior year and wonder how she will manage student teaching just as her final season of Big Ten play heads into high gear.

Practice remains flat again today. During the Continuous Lay-up Drill, players botch passes and shots before Coach Lee halts the action, "Karen, what do you think of our performance this morning?"

Karen is succinct, "Pretty crappy."

"We're starting practice all over again," Lee orders. "Everybody to center court."

The players return to the stretching that initiates each practice while Lee provides the commentary.

"You're going to have a good practice. You're going to start all over again. We've got to be thick-skinned, ladies. I'm going to be on you because everyone else is going to be on you this weekend. Stay with me."

Players reenact the Continuous Lay-up Drill with slight improvements in shooting and passing. During this second round of the drill,

Coach Myers has inserted an audiotaped cassette of crowd noise into the public address system. A mind-numbing blare of mixed chants and bleacher pounding pours from enormous speakers suspended above the court, a tactic coaches hope will prepare players for the high-decible noise indigenous to Wisconsin Fieldhouse.

Only thirty minutes into practice, during the Double Down Drill, players pause and lean, resting their hands against their knees as they gasp for air. I'm not sure if this is a gesture of exhaustion or resistance, but I see Tangela eye Malikah with a hard gaze and recognize growing resentment between the two. During a transition drill, play deteriorates. At one point, pursuing a rebound, Malikah collides with Tangela, knocking her to the parquet where she remains until Shannon helps her to rise. Ignoring the incident, Malikah turns and walks to the sideline, a response that infuriates Coach Lee. The crowd noise continues, and I must rely on Lee's flying arms and stiff posture to know that she is as frustrated as I have seen her. Malikah listens with a blank stare.

During a half-court scrimmage, tension escalates. Coach Lee seems nearly unable to contain her anger with players who no longer seem to care for each other or for the game. At the end of the drill, she calls Roxann onto the court. Upset that Susan is still sick, Coach Lee wants her healthy. Moments later, approaching the assistant coaches who harbor quietly at the center circle, Lee speaks briefly before departing the arena in haste. Dazed by the crowd noise and the action, I have little insight to offer Amy who, sidelined with injury and seated at my side, suddenly looks up from her math textbook to ask me what's happened. I do not know.

Ten minutes later, Coach Lee returns. She bears no sign of frustration and anger, even in the unspoken language of her body. In the meantime, Coach Myers has extinguished the crowd noise, and players have paired up for free throw shooting at the main and temporary baskets. They shoot in absolute silence. At the hoop nearest me, Nadine and Tangela are partners. In the midst of Nadine's free throw sequence, Tangela suddenly walks off court, where she crouches and begins quietly to cry. I look hard to make sure I'm seeing right, for the response is one I've never seen. Because Nadine chooses not to intervene, I do the same. After several minutes, Tangela lifts her head from her knees and returns to the free throw line, where Nadine, standing pensive, waits for her. We are the only ones who have witnessed the moment.

Coach Lee calls the team to center court for one last drill. Her countenance remains upbeat. Referring to her written scouting report of Penn State, Lee asks, "One question. Are we too tired to run through this?" The players uniformly answer no, except for Tiffany who seems to hedge.

"Tiffany?" Lee asks.

Tiffany's response is so muffled I cannot discern it, but whatever the remark, it seems to register with Karen who retorts, "Come on, you're acting like you're tired. Let's go."

Things have indeed fallen apart for this squad. Karen struggles amidst personal difficulties to lead a team torn by dissension. Simone's rehabilitation has exiled her to training rooms in and beyond the arena. Malikah has grown tired of injury and resentful of those who play. Tangela wallows in a shooting slump and believes that players and coaches hold her accountable for too much of the team's success. Other players are distracted by family struggles, personal relationships, and the demands of school. And coaches have lost a sense for how to restore players' confidence in themselves and trust in each other.

The night before Friday's contest with Penn State, Coach Lee announces a mandatory team meeting at her home. I am not invited to the meeting and understand why. What allows players and coaches to coalesce in consciousness during moments of disintegration is the heightened intimacy that is achieved only by a sacred distinction between insider and outsider. While I have considerable access to players and coaches, I am not important enough to be recognized during liminal moments such as this. On the eve of a game that will do much to determine the Big Ten championship, this team turns in upon itself.

On Friday, the morning of the Penn State contest, I enter the arena to the rhythms of a snare drum, which Nadine has discovered in the pep band section. Malikah and Tiffany enact a lively improvisational dance, a source of comedy when Nadine shifts to cut-time. Other players gather near the home bench where, instead of sitting in isolation, they stand and chat. Shannon approaches me, noting that she has received a C+ on her Interpretive Literature paper, the one she completed on the road last weekend. She races back to the locker room to retrieve the essay so that I can review it during practice. We are both surprised at the grade, which is low for Shannon. After practice, I will try to help her interpret the instructor's comments. In the event she has received only a grade, the interpretive process will be more difficult.

Moments later, the coaches arrive and Lee greets me with a smile, "You're going on the bus tomorrow, right?"

As players stretch at center court, Lee fills me in on the team meeting, explaining that it arose from coaches' profound confusion at episodes and emotions emerging from the Purdue loss. To convey their bewilderment, the coaches had reenacted one of their postpractice coaching conferences, this time dramatizing for players their inability to interpret events of this week. After the role play, Coach Lee had asked players to respond to the drama. Now, prior to a light "walk-through" practice Friday morning, Coach Lee admits that she is unsure that any-thing was accomplished.

The walk-through, a distinctive game-day practice, involves a thor-ough review of Penn State's offenses and defenses. Reserve players are instructed to perform the offensive and defensive sets of opponents, which allows starters to acclimate their visual, tactile, and aural senses to opponents' action. Lee's introduction to each offensive set begins with its name and respective hand signal, either of which the Penn State point guard will use to initiate half-court play. At this signal, Iowa defenders must instantaneously visualize the set and forestall its out-come. Unlike other Big Ten opponents that the Hawkeyes will play twice this season, Penn State and Iowa clash tonight for the first and only time. Players will rely heavily on today's scouting report, as well as game tapes they have viewed on their own time during the week.

Throughout the walk-through, players interrupt Coach Lee's nar-ration to solicit specific information on opponents' shooting ranges, preferred shots, and trademark moves. As I watch, I notice that play-ers' relationships with each other have changed. Malikah, embodying the moves of a Nittany Lion center, assists Tangela to acculturate at the low post.

Hours later, the Hawkeyes reconvene in Carver-Hawkeye Arena where they defeat the Nittany Lions 81–69. The victory is special given Penn State was the preseason pick to win the Big Ten title with Iowa slated for fourth place. Sealing this victory, the team has also succeeded in notching a payback for every loss of the 1994–1995 season. Among players, coaches, and managers, the Purdue loss had spawned a liminal week characterized by tension, fear, and confusion. What strikes me about this period is the extent to which players' emotions precipitated both disintegration and reintegration.

The Significance of Emotion and Feeling

Scholarship on embodiment is only just beginning to consider the manner in which emotion influences the interrelation of body and mind. From his work with patients who have experienced damage to the frontal lobe of the brain either by accident, tumor, or lesion, Uni-versity of Iowa neurologist Antonio Damasio claims that the experi-ence of affect is central to reason and consciousness. In his most re-cent book *The Feeling of What Happens: Body and Emotion in the Making of Consciousness*, Damasio offers compelling evidence that one's affective function has a biological constitution oriented toward regulation of the mind–body partnership. Damasio's theory of consciousness rests upon a fundamental distinction between "emotion" and "feeling." An "emotion," according to Damasio, represents a complex and distinct neurochemical response to a particular "inducing situation," or pattern of stimuli. He writes,

> The biological function of emotion is twofold. The first function is the production of a specific reaction to the inducing situation. . . . The second biological function of emotion is the regulation of the internal state of the organism such that it can be prepared for the specific reaction. For example, providing increased blood flow to arteries in the legs so that muscles receive extra oxygen and glucose, in the case of a flight reaction. . . . (1999, 52)

Here, Damasio alters our conventional understanding of emotion by disputing the traditional view that it undermines reason and consciousness. Instead, Damasio suggests that emotion serves a primary role, that of sustaining the homeostatic function of brain and body. According to Damasio, the neurochemical effect of an emotion is manifest in particular reflexes or conditioned responses that may be observable to others when they involve musculoskeletal changes in posture, facial expression, or body comportment. But these observable changes in countenance are only the visible outcomes of more consequential changes in inner body state.

For Damasio, "feeling" represents another level of body-brain regulation and occurs when an individual *recognizes* her emotional response. According to Damasio, this capacity to feel, or know, one's emotion is central to comprehension and rationality. When one possesses the "wordless knowledge" of her emotion, she is positioned to understand and make inferences about the images that enter her mind. Over time, recurring experiences of stimuli can elicit emotions for which she can feel much attachment (or not). And, over time, she grows sensitive to how the images she experiences induce the particular emotions she feels, a regulatory process that grounds subjective agency. According to Damasio,

> The fabric of our minds and our behavior is woven around continuous cycles of emotions followed by feelings that become known and beget new emotions, a running polyphony that underscores and punctuates specific thoughts in our minds and actions in our behavior. (1999, 43)

What is striking about sufferers of frontal lobe damage is how their inability to feel leads to dramatic impairments in the ability to reason and to make inferences about the contexts in which they find themselves.

Damasio's work is important for two reasons. First, he offers compelling evidence of a body–brain partnership. Second, he establishes that the experience of emotion is central to the regulation of the body and mind. While those who theorize embodiment as a cultural phenomenon may worry about the potential for biological determinism here, Damasio does maintain that the biochemical experience of emotion is shaped by cultural influence. In *Descartes' Error: Emotion, Reason, and the Human Brain*, he writes,

> I am not attempting to reduce social phenomena to biological phenomena, but rather to discuss the powerful connection between them. It should be clear that although culture and civilization arise from the behavior of biological individuals, the behavior was generated in collectives of individuals interacting in specific environments. Culture and civilization could not have arisen from single individuals and thus cannot be reduced to biological mechanisms and, even, less, can they be reduced to a subset of genetic specifications. Their comprehension demands not just general biology and neurobiology but the methodologies of the social sciences as well. (1994, 124)

For many in the social sciences, recent surges in genetic research are cause for worry. Will a mapped human genome revitalize eugenic thought? Will certain forms of being and knowing matter more than others? Damasio's theory of consciousness, in insisting upon the role of culture and the plasticity of the body–brain relationship, defies essentialization of the human gene. Promoting the interdependence of mind, body, and culture, Damasio's work is a direct threat to those who continue to invest in the longstanding argument that cognition operates apart from culture.

Following the Purdue loss, Iowa players clearly experienced affective patterns and shifts that influenced their learning. Whatever the emotions that the Purdue loss may have generated for team members, each seemed for much of the week not to "feel" it. What may be most significant about the rituals that shape learning for players and coaches, including the communal meeting on the eve of the Penn State contest, is that through ritual we are reacquainted with patterns of stimuli that engender the neurochemical response from which consciousness emerges. I suspect that rituals in any context become sacred when the images that create them induce conditioned emotions we recognize as feelings and subsequently rely upon to know, reason, and learn. In the same way, rituals in any context may become profane, triggering emotions that, whether we feel them or not, undermine teaching and learning.

As I've watched this week unfold, I am ever more convinced that emotion and feeling influence the relation of body and mind. In the twenty-four hour period preceding the Penn State victory, Iowa players experience a radical shift in affect, which results in perhaps their most impressive victory yet. Against the Nittany Lions, four Iowa starters score in double figures, and Iowa's trademark defensive press limits Penn State to 28 percent shooting in a first half for which they muster just 22 points. On both ends of the floor, the Hawkeye women have revived systemic balance.

From Body to Mind:
The Significance of Image Schemata

The morning after the Penn State win, I enter Carver-Hawkeye through the rear service entrance, where I find managers in command. Jeremy wheels a cart filled with potato chips, fruit, crackers, and soda to the bus while Nealie confirms that baggage and medical supplies are in order. The loading process is efficient and within 30 minutes, players, coaches, and support personnel have boarded. The coaches occupy seats at the front of the bus while players, one every two seats, recline with snacks. From Iowa City, the trip to Madison will last three and a half hours. After roll call, Coach Myers reads aloud the titles of videotapes housed in a small cardboard box at the front of the bus. Garnishing a slim majority vote, *Billy Madison* is the film of choice. Inserting the tape into a videocassette recorder located in an overhead cabin, Coach Myers calls for players' confirmation that, indeed, the various video monitors suspended from front to rear are in working order. Only Simone, who resides in the last row, calls out for volume. Coaches Lee and Peeples have already tuned out the noise, preferring instead to read. Once the movie is underway, Coach Myers returns to her seat and enters into sleep. The trip will offer her some reprieve from the orchestration of lodging, meals, and transportation. Hours from now and just miles from Madison, she will wake without cue to resume her duties.

During the drive, I enjoy the scenery. Conversations with players can wait; they are tired and pass quickly into sleep or study. Along Highway 151 to Dubuque, frozen fields, shorn of their soybeans and corn, slumber underneath islands of snow. Today, in bright sun, the land is a patchwork of color. Though dull in hue, the fields are impressive in scope, extending to a distant plain where earth becomes sky. For rural Iowans, the horizon means everything in winter. The danger in violent blizzards is the sudden discovery that the line has redrawn itself to the very tracks of one's feet. In winter, what seems peripheral on the upper middle plains is inevitably protean and often dangerous. I am reminded of Mari Sandoz's *Winter Thunder* and remain grateful that for passengers on this bus, at least, the trip is uneventful. As we cross the Mississippi River, I note that nearly all players and coaches are asleep, except for Simone, who makes her way to the videocassette recorder. Removing *Billy Madison,* she inserts *Apollo 13,* a selection that seems appropriate.

In so many ways Simone's voyage across cultures has been profound, a journey that has unfolded largely without navigators and without notice. A native of Jamaica, Simone came to the University of Iowa from a junior college in Oklahoma, where at 6'4" she had been recruited from Kingston not to play but *to learn* the game. During the 1994–1995 season, she had suffered her first knee injury, for which the NCAA had granted her a "medical redshirt," an opportunity to rehabilitate the remainder of the season without losing her year of eligibility. In this her senior year, Simone had finally cracked the starting line-up. But long before she could savor success, injury catapulted her into purgatory once more. The beneficiary of a second consecutive medical redshirt, Simone endures a now-familiar regimen of exercise and therapy.

Shortly before dusk, our Tri-State Tours bus arrives at a Sheraton hotel removed from the University of Wisconsin campus. Nealie and Jeremy operate in sync, assisting the driver to whisk luggage and supplies from the undercarriage. The evening schedule will afford coaches, players, and managers little free time. Following dinner in the hotel, they will convene in Coach Lee's hotel room to study game tape. Bodies will occupy every patch of floor, chair, and bed space as they attend to Coach Lee's "pause and play" commentary. On this particular evening, I leave the hotel. My younger sister, a graduate student at the University of Wisconsin, will be my host, at least until I rejoin the Hawkeye women on Sunday morning. The game in Madison is cause for a family reunion as my brother, a women's basketball fan, has traveled from Rochester, Minnesota, to join us.

On Sunday, the Wisconsin Fieldhouse fills to what will be an over-capacity crowd. A classic basketball barn, the Fieldhouse is in its last year of intercollegiate service, awaiting the completion of the multi-million dollar Kohl Center. Public universities have little use these days for arenas that seat fewer than 15,000 fans, particularly when individual endowments and corporate sponsorships buy more space for sport. With an 11,500 person capacity, the Wisconsin Fieldhouse has survived longer than most.

In a tightly packed crowd at the southeast entrance, I clutch my younger sister, fearful at the prospect of separation but nostalgic at the opportunity to attend one of the final intercollegiate contests here. Fans dressed in cardinal and white Badger regalia surround us, and small clusters of Hawkeye visitors, layered in black and gold, advance slowly amidst inadvertent jostling. Often the butt of benign teasing for their "bumble bee" attire, the Hawkeye fans in attendance today, mainly senior citizens, progress with a quiet dignity. Their Hawkeyes bring a 21–2 record to Madison and lead Wisconsin by one game in the chase for the Big Ten title.

Gradually, my sister, brother, and I find our seat, a crude bleacher several rows behind the Hawkeyes' bench. Parents, support staff, and former players have already arrived. To make room for us, they must squeeze together, which they do without hesitation. Aside from this group, the only other pocket of Iowa fans resides in the far corner of the rectangular upper balcony, where their effect on crowd noise will certainly be neglible. Minutes before the tip-off, the noise in the Wisconsin Fieldhouse begins a crescendo that will not peak until the final seconds. Perhaps the audiotaped crowd noise that has accompanied practices this week will have prepared Iowa players. Or perhaps playing on the road for the first time since Purdue will rekindle insecurities. Whatever the outcome, Karen's performance will be crucial. As a senior, she has had three years to acclimate to time, space, and situation. As a point guard, she initiates and sustains ball movement during offensive sets. Beside knowing the plays, Karen must know her players. She must know how they post, jump, pass, screen, and move in order to facilitate the most rapid and secure rotation of the ball. Most importantly, Karen must be prepared to adjust her understanding when players depart, by injury or volition, from bodily activity she expects. While each player understands their activity and thought as contingent upon others, Karen initiates the plays that will take fullest advantage of what her teammates know and can do each game.

The Cultivation of Image Schemata

To understand how Karen "knows" one must accept that what she knows is inarguably a condition of how and where she learns. Herein lies a problem. While understanding the relationship of cognitive structures to bodily place is central to this analysis of learning as embodied, documenting their interrelationship poses methodological problems. According to Damasio, so little is known about the interrelation of body and brain that researchers must rely "on a natural human ability, that of theorizing constantly about the state of mind of others from observations of behaviors, reports of mental states, and counterchecking of their correspondences, given one's own comparable experiences" (1999, 83–84). Though the triangulation of theory, observation, and personal anecdote may invoke criticism from many in the hard sciences, Damasio acknowledges its merit.

Today, against Wisconsin, Karen's bodily activity will facilitate the successful progression of the ball from player to player and from player to basket. As a senior point guard and starter for two seasons, she is a master of what Johnson terms the *path schema*, a cognitive structure that orients her to the progressive rotation of the ball across court space. Karen's reliance upon the path schema has temporal limits attuned both to the 30 second shot clock and the game clock. At one point in the season, I had watched Karen dribble the ball upcourt during a scrimmage. By mistake, a manager had activated the shot clock several seconds before the start of action, leaving Karen with fewer seconds than her regulation 30. At the sound of the buzzer, a full three seconds early, Karen turned to the manager's table with an emphatic "the clock was off." Indeed, it was. And Karen seemed to have "felt" so. Later, she explained her response,

> Part of my responsibility that's been driven into my head over the years, among other things, is how much time I have on the clock. I think after you run a certain number of plays and you run them as many times as we do, knowing you have to be aware of time, I think you know. If a ball has swung around two or three times, then your time has to be running short. You know if it goes off early. There's no way that's right.

As Karen described it, the path schema involves a full-court awareness for the ball's orientation to players and to the basket, all within strict dimensions of time. Karen must keep the ball rotating through the various positions on the court until an open shot is available. In effect, all players, not just Karen, are responsible for rotating the ball to a position on the floor from which the highest percentage shot can be attempted. For systemic balance to occur, each player must be prepared to take the shot when it becomes available. From the equilibrium of the ball itself, to the stable distribution of a player's body weight, to the homeostatic nature of offensive and defensive sets, balance is primary. Karen's job is to initiate and regulate play so that the pursuit of balance is possible.

In addition to Karen, the remaining Iowa starters—Tangela, Nadine, Tiffany, and Shannon—will also rely upon the containment schema. Concretely, participants are aware of boundaries to the court as a whole. To step "out of bounds" is to simultaneously lose possession of the ball and the chance to score. A comprehensive sense of court space is considered so fundamental to the game that players have little excuse for a violation as basic to court sense as "stepping on the line." More specifically, though, players refine containment schema in accordance with their designated positions on the floor. In this way, containment means different things at different positions.

For post players, the containment schema is primary. Amy, Jenny, Malikah, Simone, and Tangela occupy the lane, a rectangular space that surrounds the hoop. As defenders, the task of these players is to deny the ball from entering this space, where the shooting percentages of opponents are often highest. Containment is achieved when defensive post players orient toward the axial condition "out" by filling passing lanes and interrupting the possibility that opposing players on the perimeter can pass the ball to teammates in the lane. Containing the ball to the perimeter, or keeping it "out," also involves various schemata for force. Posts rely upon a wide stance, low hips, and solid shoulder blocks as they front, play behind or three-quarter their offensive opponents. Such defensive stances allow post defenders to exert the force necessary to forestall opponents' rolls, cuts, pins, and screens, all maneuvers designed for offensive players to get open. When they shift to offense, and must position themselves to score, Iowa posts will reorient their axial understanding of containment to privilege body and ball movement that progress "in." They must anticipate and counter the containment and force schemata used against them in an effort to create passing lanes that will allow the ball entrance to the lane.

For most basketball players, the containment schema is activated even before play begins. Pregame rituals that may appear merely ceremonial to spectators actually hold abstract significance, engendering as they do the image schemata that will be required on court. What makes the huddle such a symbolic ritual in team sport is that the experience of space is nearly identical for each participant. Oriented equidistant from a center point, each member's axial experience of space and other is the same. No player occupies a space with more frontal vision than another, and each is included in the frontal vision of those in her midst. Aside from being the most egalitarian and relational of rituals, the enclosure also sharpens the distinction between insider and outsider. The geometry of the huddle is universally significant in sport because it encourages players to affirm the abstract orientation necessary for team play. Players see, feel, and constitute a relational unit for which no single player is supreme. Whether or not the huddle triggers this orientation depends, of course, upon one's investment not just in the ritual but in her teammates and coaches.

Of those Iowa players starting the game, I cannot guess who will assume leadership today. I will not have to wait long to discover that Tangela's start will again be slow. Within eleven minutes of the opening jump and with just two points, Tangela commits her third foul. She is called to the bench, where she will remain the rest of the half. On the sidelines, Tangela joins freshman reserve players Amy and Stacy. Typical of freshman, these players are still acculturating to the schemata expected of them on court. As individuals, each must learn not only the host of schemata central to her position but, as a player in relation to others, she must also internalize the schemata required at the other four positions. Only in this way can a team synchronize its actions offensively and defensively. In short, learning requires not just isolated knowledge of all play options at one's own position but a comprehensive sense for the full potentiality of play.

At several points during the season, I have observed the developmental spurts of Amy and Stacy, freshman players at the post and point guard positions, respectively. During one practice, Coach Lee repositioned players to test their knowledge of the offense. With Tangela, a post, looming at the point guard position and Amy, also a post, shifted out to the wing, Coach Lee had ordered Stacy, a point guard, to the post position near the hoop. Within seconds of the first offensive play, Stacy and Amy were lost. Coach Lee made her point, "Stacy and Amy, you two are a treat! It's obvious you only know your own little world. I mean I've got Tangela up here running the gamut." Later, Tangela spoke about the significance of Coach Lee's drill.

> In a sense, everybody has to know what everybody else does. That's why when Stacy and I were on the court, and Stacy was going through the plays in her head like she does before every game, and I said, "Okay, what does the post do in this play?," she said, "I don't know what the post player does!" Karen and I were like, " . . . You're supposed to know what everybody does." I said, "I know what the guards do when we do the plays, so you gotta know what the posts do." She's like, "Okay. Okay." So I asked her, "Where does the post go in such and such a play?" And she was like, "I don't know!" She didn't even know.

The lesson of Coach Lee's drill was clear. For the Hawkeye women, no single player and no single schematic orientation is—in and of itself—"the world." In fact, to only know "your own little world" is to know nothing at all. Conceptually, one is never simply a forward or a guard. Bodily activity is not only referential to one's positional schemata, it is referential to a comprehensive network of schemata. Though learning involved the interpretation of positional knowledge as it is taught by coaches and elder players, the goal is intersubjectivity, that capacity to move beyond introspection to a reflexive understanding of oneself through the activity of others.

At the heart of the Wisconsin team are All-American candidates at the point guard and post positions. They take quick advantage of Tangela's absence by spreading play wide enough that passing lanes take on the look of autobahns. What I find striking about Tangela's play is her nearly singular reliance upon the containment schema. While force schemata require the resistance to or imposition of power upon another human being, the containment schema orients an individual not

toward another human being but to the boundary between ball and opponent. Using speed and agility, Tangela is often able to fill a passing
lane without the need for force. Her foul trouble today is unusual and
will pose a risk to Iowa's renowned full- and half-court press. Within
range of becoming Iowa's all-time leader for blocked shots, Tangela's
presence in the lane also imposes upon the vertical leap of opponents.
In her absence, it is no surprise that Wisconsin posts reorient their activity in the lane.

As action intensifies, Arneda and Tia, two players from the Final
Four squad, lead our small Iowa contingent in a cheer so muted it barely
reaches the Iowa bench. Still, the two stand and flail, joined by Susan's
father, a kind-faced gentleman who responds less with zeal than with
pure elation. From the team bench, Iowa coaches signal play sequences
to Karen by the flash of a cue card, which she reads on her up court
dribble and signals by hand to teammates. At the end of the first half,
Tiffany and Shannon have managed to keep Iowa in the game, and
Karen, though she has not scored a point, has sustained offensive
rotations.

At halftime the score is tied. As Iowa players proceed to the locker
room, coaches gather in a circle near the Iowa bench to confer. Briefly,
they analyze stat sheets the managers have provided them. From this
data, they compare individual and team statistics, considering the adjustments in activity that will be necessary in the coming half. From
her assistants, Coach Lee confirms her own ideas and synthesizes comments she finds relevant. From this process of conferral will come her
halftime presentation to players, for whom she will provide specific recommendations and solicit questions.

For Karen, the second half of this game will mean reassessing
Tangela and Nadine. Will they recoup? Because neither Tangela nor
Nadine responds to angry prompts, coaches and teammates will do
everything possible to reassure the two at halftime. More than criticism, they need faith. If the attempts to engender it fail, the game will
rest upon increased shots from Tiffany, Shannon, Karen, as well as
those who substitute into the game. With that prospect, new questions
arise. Will Tiffany's knee sustain the elevation she needs for her jump-
shot throughout the remainder of the game? Will reserves sitting cold
on the bench adjust quickly to action? Karen must consider all this
during halftime. This season, injuries, position changes, and wavering
levels of confidence have complicated assessment.

As the teams return to the court and engage in warm-up shooting,
Tangela and Nadine focus their attention exclusively on the basket.
They do not interact with teammates or with each other. During the
first five minutes of the half, action is again frenetic. The multiple lead
changes continue. This half, though, Nadine and Tangela are sinking

shots. With 11:58 remaining, Wisconsin center Barb Franke commits her fourth foul and is called to the bench. Her departure provides Iowa players an opportunity for which they must take advantage, but back-to-back three-point plays by Keisha Anderson frustrate the attempt.

At the ten-minute mark, Tangela finds a rhythm she will not relinquish. She is "in the zone," the term players use to note the onset of the highest level of consciousness. Feeding off each other's success, Nadine and Tangela liberate themselves of the self-consciousness that stifled their first-half play. They are no longer fixated upon carrying out the activity of their respective positions. They perform not as isolated selves but as part of a systemic whole. What Tangela does in the lane now compliments what Nadine performs on the perimeter and vice versa. While Tiffany, Karen, and Shannon may not match Tangela and Nadine in scoring, they sustain the ball rotation central to systemic balance. In the final minutes, each player thinks and moves with a reflexive understanding of what is possible across the entire court.

At the 2:37 mark, Nadine scores nine straight points. The score is 63–59 and while the Iowa players float across the court, opening themselves to a "multiradial" understanding of person and place, the Badgers progress by sheer mechanical will. They do not give up, but they do not seem to invent themselves either. The contrast in play is dramatic.

With 1:49 remaining, the score is tied at 63. Together, Tangela and Nadine account for all Iowa's second half points. They have oriented to court space in the Naismith tradition. From beyond the three-point scoring line, Nadine's perimeter shooting has expanded the Iowa offense, drawing Wisconsin players farther and farther from the basket. As opponents' reliance upon the containment schema weakens, Tangela has room to maneuver and score.

At the 50 seconds mark, Tangela scores off a feed from Karen to edge Iowa ahead by two. During the next offensive sequence for Wisconsin, a Badger player misfires from the wing, and the two small clusters of Iowa fans seem already to know that Nadine will snake through the lane to snare the rebound and feed it to Karen. Eyeing the clock, Karen knows that ball rotation and scoring must coincide with temporal limits. In the final seconds either Nadine or Tangela must have the ball. Every observer in the Fieldhouse is standing now.

The Iowa players continue to coordinate their movements of ball and body. With 18 seconds left, Karen receives the ball at the top of the key and rotates it inside to Tangela, who is fouled on the pass. Though she is not fouled in the act of shooting, Tangela has earned a one-and-one opportunity, a chance to increase the Iowa lead to four points. As players take their places around the lane, I worry that the delay may disrupt Tangela, who stands at the free throw line facing baseline bleachers filled with jeering Wisconsin fans. Seconds later, her first shot bounces off the glass, rebounded by an opponent who quickly initiates an outlet pass to Keisha.

Just seconds are left now, and action unfolds as if in slow motion. Karen guards Keisha tightly, preempting a three-point attempt and forcing Keisha to pass the ball to the wing. In a hurried shot with six seconds remaining, the wing player elevates to shoot. At the same time, from several feet away, Tangela catapults her body into the trajectory of the ball. With her right arm extended, her 6'4" frame ascends until somehow she is able to bat the ball from space. In the process, Tangela retrieves the ball and is fouled.

Four seconds remain. Iowa leads 65–63. Again, play stops so that teams can assemble at the far free throw line. In the meantime, crowd noise reaches its crescendo. Wisconsin fans know Tangela has missed once, and they will do their most to distract her a second time. The combination of a rebound, four seconds, and Keisha Anderson make anything possible. Wisconsin requires two points to tie and three to win.

Again, Tangela must wait for players to assemble around the lane. At decibels that are almost painful, crowd noise reverberates off person and place. Tangela receives the ball from the referee and releases another one-and-one opportunity. I know from its arc that the shot is off. I want to close my eyes, but as the ball leaves the glass, I see that Jenny, whom coaches have substituted in for her height advantage, has not been blocked out by her defender. As the ball caroms off the rim and descends in her direction, Jenny remains open to the ball, the result of a defensive error so elementary I cannot believe what I see. But what I see is real. Wisconsin defenders have made the mistake of jumping toward a ball that will pass above and beyond their reach. At a point in space that spectators seem to anticipate, Jenny rises to the ball. Before she can be fouled, she pitches the ball outside the lane to Nadine. A high percentage free-throw shooter, Nadine will take the foul with a second remaining and sink the final two points of the game. Iowa defeats Wisconsin 67–63.

At the buzzer, Iowa reserves and coaches break onto the floor. In their mad race to each other, they bypass opponents who must wait to offer ceremonial high fives. The oversight prompts Wisconsin fans to boo, but the Iowa team is already so lost in joy they do not notice either their *faux pas* or the response. Iowa players have gathered in a collective huddle at center court. Seconds later they turn outward to offer effusive waves and blown kisses to fans in the rafters. Defeating the Wisconsin Badgers amidst a record capacity of 11,522, the team has earned a share of the Big Ten title.

The celebration continues after players have showered and rejoined fans at a postgame party hosted by the I-Club affiliate in Wisconsin. As the team arrives in the Mendota Gridiron Room, located adjacent to Camp Randall Stadium, Coach Lee leaps onto a banquet table where she offers effusive credit to the Iowa "family," a term reserved for those who play and those who follow. Suddenly, the clusters that seemed paltry jam the banquet room. In my claustrophobia, I pull my brother and sister to the door, where we listen to coaches and players take turns thanking fans. Nadine and Tangela join the celebration late, having spent extra time with a press corps that seized upon Nadine's career-high 31 points, including five out of seven three-pointers, and Tangela's 15 second-half points and five blocked shots, including three in the final minutes. To the reporter who posed a question about the Wisconsin fans, Tangela remarked, "I put it in my mind that they were cheering for us not against us."

The Extension of Image Schemata into Metaphor

Tangela's comment signals another means by which participants in this study made meaning. In addition to their reliance upon image schemata, players often activate a network of figurative meaning. In this instance, Tangela employed a strategy that is common in sport and involves the conceptual manipulation of person and place. Superimposing a sense for home onto her experience of this foreign site and audience, Tangela initiated a schematic shift. In effect, she remakes place by reimagining the experience of force. For participants in this study, metaphorical projections involving the concept of house, or home, were prevalent. Their frequency is not surprising given, as Gaston Bachelard (1969) notes, that "the house is one of the greatest powers of integration for the thoughts, memories, and dreams of mankind" (6). Not uncommonly, one hears basketball players allude to their "house" or "home," a reference either to their positions on the court or to their native arenas. Earlier in the season, as Malikah was explaining her responsibilities as a post, she had noted,

> My mindset is that that yellow paint right there is mine. You know, they say "my house." Don't let nobody in that you don't want to be there. Treat it like it's your house. If somebody's in there scoring, you can't let them do that. You got to get them out because they're messing with your house, just tryin' to run your house. I think it's an authoritative attitude as far as a shot or as far as handling the ball. I think when you're a post, you have an authoritative attitude toward certain areas on the court. . . . You can't be a baby in there and every time somebody hits you, you get mad. You've got to enjoy contact. You're in a space that's about 12' by 15'. And that's where all the action is taking place.

Here, Malikah makes reference to the acts of force and containment central to her play in the lane. Her schema for containment seems to extend into an existing network of figurative meaning for which she holds considerable affect. Over the several years that I watched Malikah and her teammates on court, I began to understand the significance of this recurring conceptual metaphor. Architects Lynda Schneekloth and Robert Shibley (1995) have examined the act of "placemaking" and write,

> The making of places—our homes, our neighborhoods, our places of work and play—not only changes and maintains the physical world of living; it also is a way we make our communities and connect with people. In other words, placemaking is not just about the relationship of people to their places, it also creates relationships among people in places. (1)

What strikes me about the extension of image schemata into existing metaphorical structures for "home" is that so long as a player feels that she contributes to the care and cultivation of place—that she helps, in effect, to define place—the metaphor of home facilitates the partnership of mind and body. As a former player, Coach Lee acknowledged, "We talk every game about how this is our house and this is a sacred place. It's nice to be able to walk through that tunnel and see the black and gold and be able to feel the bright lights. That's a warm feeling."

During the months of January and February, as Malikah grew tired of practices that did not translate into game time, her metaphorical sense for "home" disengaged from the image schemata required of her play on court. Though language can only partially reveal the profundity of metaphor, Malikah's obligatory connection to placemaking responsibilities for which she had formerly held deep regard suggested the metaphor was no longer transformative for her. At one point in February, she had remarked to me that she felt she did everything at Carver-Hawkeye Arena but sleep. Though we contemplated in jest how one might take permanent residence in the arena, I knew Malikah's exasperation pointed to a shifting response to place, a sense that the court was less about personalizing a place than about laboring to produce. While this sentiment was not to fully take root until the next competitive season, I recognized its onset at a time when the team was experiencing extraordinary success. For Malikah, the figurative attachment to place no longer arose from metaphorical extension or cultural reinforcement.

Why They Play

For participants in this study, court learning was both a bodily and conceptual process that involved the collective codification of schematic orientations to person, place, and time. Embodied schematic structures emerged from bodily activity through two processes. By means of imaginative projection, players developed schematic orientations to containment, force, verticality, balance, and motion. When a particular schema extended into existing networks of figurative meaning, players' learning was enhanced by means of metaphorical projection. Both imaginative and metaphorical projection constituted pathways to embodied cognition. The emergence of mental structures from concrete bodily experience demanded considerable time, instruction, and practice and was facilitated by rituals that possessed affective significance for players. Given the central role of affect in moments of disintegration and reintegration, Damasio's (1994, 1999) claim that emotion plays a neurochemical role central to the regulation of mind and body warrants the ongoing attention of those scholars and practitioners who document embodied cognition.

For the Iowa Hawkeyes, the 1995–1996 conference season ended with victories against Michigan and Illinois. With a record of 15–1 in Big Ten play, Iowa earned sole possession of the conference title. During postseason NCAA tournament play, the University of Iowa hosted first and second round action, defeating Butler and DePaul to progress to the Mideast Regional bracket in Chicago, where the the team faced #12 Vanderbilt. Against the Commodores, the Iowa women would repeat the habit of their season. Down at the half 34–16, they would not recover, despite perimeter shooting from Nadine and Tiffany. With a 74–63 loss, the Iowa women finished their season at 27–4 and received a #7 ranking in the final AP poll.

At the public banquet held in honor of players and coaches in April, the team continued the program's tradition of not identifying individual players for achievement. No most valuable or most improved players were announced. For those in attendance, this seemed appropriate. The 1995–1996 season seemed less about singular achievements than about the inexhaustible effort and desire of players and coaches to negotiate an identity at a time when few if any were predicting such an outcome. What struck me most about the everyday court learning of players was the degree to which they weathered challenges without relinquishing primary interest in their welfare as a collective whole. On no occasion when a player was ordered to run alone did I not find others joining voluntarily. As Jenny explained to me,

> . . . that's just something that's understood. If one of your teammates has to run alone, somebody's going to run with them. . . . It's just understood that someone's going to join up with them after they catch their breath or whatever because we know it's hard to do that by yourself. To be out there having to make this time. And nobody's pushing you and you just feel like dying. And everybody's standing there getting water. I find that when I'm running a sprint that I don't have to run, it's fine. I don't care. I mean, I'll run it and no complaints because I didn't have to run it. It was under my control. Yeah, I think it's just

the support factor. They'd be there for me. They've been there for me,
so I'm going to be there for them on this one.

The schematic structures that players relied upon in the concrete enactment of their bodily activity seemed to configure their abstract understanding of place and person. In quiet ways, on and off the court,
players' activity reaffirmed the sentiment they often noted in words.
With just four losses across nearly 30 games, the Iowa Hawkeyes had
sustained systemic balance across nearly an entire season of play. To
do so, they had relied upon levels of trust and mutual support rarely
achieved in other contexts of learning.

Chapter Four

Academic Integrity
The Need for "Live Encounters"

Academic institutions offer myriad ways to protect ourselves from the threat of a live encounter. To avoid a live encounter with teachers, students can hide behind their notebooks and their silence. To avoid a live encounter with students, teachers can hide behind their podiums, their credentials, and their power. To avoid a live encounter with one another, faculty can hide behind their academic specialties. . . . To avoid a live encounter with subjects of study, teachers and students alike can hide behind the pretense of objectivity: students can say, "Don't ask me to think about this stuff—just give me the facts," and faculty can say, "Here are the facts—don't think about them, just get them straight."

Parker J. Palmer,
The Courage to Teach (1997)

Compositionist Donna Qualley maintains that several conditions are necessary for reflexive thought to occur in any context of learning. These features include engagement with an other, opportunities to maintain dialogue and negotiate perception, a sense of agency, and an emphasis on understanding, not just knowledge (1997, 20–23). For the female athletes, these features emerged from a series of hermeneutical relationships that included mind–body, self–other, and structure–antistructure. While some may argue that reflexive understanding is

79

not something postsecondary institutions should feel bound to foster, I maintain that opportunities for students to use a wider range of mental schemata represent a fundamental commitment to conceptual diversity. The problem, of course, is that public universities, oriented the past half-century toward the mass matriculation of undergraduates, now depend on academic programs, policies, and pedagogies that mitigate against reflexivity. In this chapter I consider how the "live encounters" central to the negotiation of perception and reflexive consciousness are preempted in the academic domain by the reliance on lecture-based general education courses, undersupported graduate instructors, and redundant remediation programs. As I note later in this chapter, recent cases of academic fraud at institutions across the country do indeed underscore the need for ambitious athletic reform. Nonetheless, holding intercollegiate athletic departments largely responsible for the decline of academic integrity (NAFCAR 2000, Sperber 2000) is both unfair and uncritical. Troublesome features of learning characterize both academic and athletic domains.

The Absence of "Live Encounters"

This chapter is grounded in the context of my own ten-year history in various institutional spaces designed to support academic learning at the University of Iowa. In 1986, I began work as a writing tutor in the Office of Athletic Student Services, a retention program housed in the men's athletic department. In 1993, I assumed a two-year teaching assistantship in the first-year rhetoric program, and in 1994, I accepted additional duties in the Writing Center. These years of overlapping service in multiple sites acquainted me with institutional features that restrict ways of knowing available to students in the academic domain. At issue is what I call *schematic portability*, which refers to the degree schemata learners rely on in one context are available to them in another. Concern for schematic portability is a way of identifying the conceptual disjunctures students face as they traverse multiple sites of learning within a single institution. In this chapter, I consider the academic learning of members of the Iowa women's basketball team in the broader context of my own instructional history during a decade when institutional reliance on NCAA legislation did little to encourage the legitimate scrutiny of prohibitive academic structures. I conclude with recommendations designed to support the conceptual diversity of students who make knowledge in ways traditionally overlooked in college classrooms.

The Problem of Disembodiment in General Education Courses

In their lecture-based courses, student athletes in this study had few opportunities to draw on the embodied mental structures they employed on court. Like their undergraduate peers, the women in this study spent significant periods of their academic learning in lecture halls that seated fifty to three hundred students. Where learning was characterized by the transmission of information, students' knowledge-making was disassociated from concrete activity and interaction in ways that proved difficult for some in this study to reconcile. As Jenny noted,

> I cannot sit in a lecture hall and watch the teacher put notes up on the overhead. . . . Just going pretty much from what he's gotten written up there. I can't do it because there's no interaction. If it's a small discussion group, a class of maybe fifteen or twenty people, I think I do much better because I can give my point of view and hear what other people say. And hearing what other people think, whatever you're studying, is like, "Oh, God, now I understand. They were confused on that, too, and they figured out a way to understand it."

The vital partnership of mind and body and the collective cultivation of embodied schemata so important to athletic learning were relatively useless in lecture-based classrooms. In these courses, cognition often hinged solely on "propositional" schemata (Johnson 1987), those mental structures that allowed learners to process the symbolic activity of an instructor. In this way, the solitary knowing demanded of learners in lecture hall formats reflected traditional assumptions about cognition as a psychological condition requiring only linguistic mediation.

The disembodied nature of learning in general education courses seems ironic in light of the central importance of embodied schemata to intellectual discovery. Robert and Michele Root-Bernstein (2000) argue that "the kind of thinking in every discipline that generates and conceptualizes new insights—relies on . . . images, patterns, sensual and muscular feelings, play-acting, empathizing, emotions, and intuitions" (A64). They point out the curious insistence on the primacy of propositional structures as the means to understanding when, in fact, creative discovery and imagination rely so often on bodily activity. Of the irony, they write, "Those forms of knowledge have almost no place in our universities, where thinking is almost universally presented as if formal logic were its basis, and words and mathematics its language of choice" (2000, A64). For the women in this study, the lack of schematic portability across sites of learning was most pronounced in lecture-hall formats. From the bodily activity that characterized their relational play on the basketball court emerged embodied mental structures central to reflexive understanding. In the classroom, however, linguistic activity demanded sole reliance on propositional schemata, those mental structures supporting solitary thought.

First-Year Composition and the Inequities of Being

Accorded the responsibility of first-year composition instruction, the department of rhetoric at the University of Iowa solicited its graduate instructors from the wider university. Because the department lacked its own Ph.D. program, it relied on a multidisciplinary staff of over 100 graduate students. As a teaching assistant in the mid-1990s, I found that the three days of instructor training prior to each school year did little to assuage the anxiety of those who felt ill-equipped to teach and assess writing. By "teach writing," I refer to the rich and variegated theoretical traditions in composition studies (Berlin 1988), as well as the theorized pedagogies that have emerged from these traditions. While each semester included weekly advisory sessions in which teaching assistants met in groups with designated tenure stream rhetoric faculty, many instructors, for reasons of angst and understandable need, relied on these sessions for quick-fixes.

For two sections of composition that met four days a week, graduate instructors received no tuition reimbursement, health benefits, or merit recognition. Nearly half of my $1,100 monthly salary returned to the university as tuition payment. Making ends meet during my doctoral study required two additional jobs. It was during this period when my tutorial relationship with Tangela began. Throughout her first year, as I taught and she learned in the two-semester rhetoric sequence, I listened to her accounts of instructors and recognized myself.

> With a lot of teachers it's like every two seconds they are looking at their watches. Sometimes it just feels like a rush job. I can tell they just want to get it over with and be done with me. This makes it hard for me to concentrate. It's already hard because I'm very shy. I have a hard time expressing how I'm feeling without thinking that I'm going to ask a dumb question.

Labor conditions at the University of Iowa were not an anomaly. Joseph Harris (2000) acknowledges that tenure stream faculty at most research institutions "have abandoned . . . basic and first-year writing . . . to an army of largely underpaid, under-trained, and under-supported teaching assistants, part-timers, and adjuncts. We have said, in effect, that almost anybody who enrolls in a graduate program in English can teach—at a reduced salary—the courses that make up the bulk of our undergraduate enrollments" (58–59).

My experiences teaching freshman composition led me to question an institutional structure that appoints those who are least trained, subsidized, and supported to instruct entry-level students. Beyond questions of expertise, I worry that the working conditions that constrain the professional and personal well-being of graduate instructors may incline them to resent the material influence of large athletic programs. Put simply, those least positioned to understand the conceptual dilemmas of student athletes are often those who are held accountable for doing so. In her analysis of teaching practices that best respond to cultural differences, Gloria Ladson-Billings (1992) maintains,

> Teachers who practice culturally relevant methods can be identified by the way they see themselves and others. . . . They see themselves as part of the community and they see teaching as giving back to the community. . . . They demonstrate a connectedness with all of their students and encourage that same connectedness between their students. Finally, such teachers are identified by their notions of knowledge: they believe that teaching is continuously re-created, recycled, and shared by students and teachers alike. (25)

The obvious paradox is that entry-level composition courses serving the full range of conceptual diversity represented on campuses are often taught by graduate students who are made to feel the least sense of community and connection. For this reason, these instructors may be unable to understand the needs of those who rely on these conditions to know and learn.

The Redundancy of Remediation

Complicating matters at Iowa, sections of a basic writing course were extinguished in the mid-1990s, part of a national trend to eliminate "remedial" courses at colleges and universities. While the course had always been unpopular with students, this was primarily its status as a zero-credit pass-fail course. With its dissolution, basic writers were mainstreamed into the general freshmen rhetoric sequence, where the onus of responsibility again fell on graduate instructors, few of whom possessed sufficient knowledge of basic writing research and theory. Harvey Wiener, former dean for academic affairs at the City University of New York, suggests that the demise of basic writing programs has disturbing implications for transitional students. Wiener predicts that the elimination of basic writing programs will escalate and that where they remain, there will exist continued reliance on instructors who lack training. As a result, he warns, demands for "reliable assessment measures" will encourage the kind of skill-and-drill instruction that has long alienated students (1998, 100–101). In *Changing the Odds: Open Admission and the Life Chances of the Disadvantaged*, David Lavin and David

Hyllegard (1996) predict that the divestiture of transitional programs will dramatically alter the cultural diversity on college campuses. I would argue the likelihood that the elimination of such programs will decrease conceptual diversity as well. While Sharon Crowley (1998) and others call for an end to first-year composition programs, Michael Murphy (2000) argues that the significant revenues garnered from courses staffed by teaching assistants, part-timers, and adjuncts insures their existence, no matter what the cost to students' and teachers' emotional and intellectual well-being.

For student athletes designated "at-risk" one of the most disturbing features of academic learning was the obligation to receive multiple layers of academic support. When I left the University of Iowa in 1997, there existed at least three independent retention programs. The Bridge Program, a required supplementary service, was housed in the College of Education and employed preservice teacher candidates. Participating students were required to attend study sessions at least twice a week. The Office of Student Services, housed in the men's athletic department, required probationary students to attend evening study tables ranging from two to four days per week. The Writing Center served those students whose first-year composition teachers recommended supplementary instruction. Separate buildings, instructional staffs, and administrative procedures presented considerable logistical and organizational demands for students already juggling extensive responsibilities to sport and school. The burden of multiple layers of remediation contributed to participants' belief that few in the academic realm understood their intellectual capacity and commitment. As Nadine remarked,

> I feel so many think we're dumb. We're not dumb. I feel that student-athletes carry two loads. We have two full-time jobs, and that's impossible to have if you ask a college man or woman. But we do it every day. We're full-time students and full-time athletes. Granted, you get tired, but you still got to do it. I want someone else to be in our shoes.

Ultimately, student athletes required to participate in multiple support programs had little time or reason to conceptualize why they were doing what they were doing and how, in the larger scheme of things, what they were doing mattered. Above all, the conditions did little to assist student athletes to challenge the dichotomous relation of their athletic and academic learning. The qualitative effect of redundant remediation underscored for student athletes just how many instructors and administrators doubted their intellectual abilities. Rather than enable students, such programming may actually heighten the resistance of those sensitive to the perception that they are "dumb."

Decade-old assertions that white athletes think and African American players feel have long infiltrated the discourse of sport. In some cases, these racist assumptions are promoted by sports commentators like former Marquette University coach Al McGuire who asserted publically that "The only thing in this country that African Americans really dominate, except poverty, is basketball" (qtd. in Telander 1995, 1). Most student athletes in high-profile sports are well aware of the racial distinctions that continue to be drawn in increasingly insidious ways between white and African American athletes. For this reason, African American student athletes enrolled in predominantly white universities often face a burden their white counterparts do not. By virtue of their embodied racial difference, they may possess a heightened degree of fear and hesitation. Billy Hawkins (1995) suggests that the powerlessness experienced by African American male and female student athletes is intensified by racial, educational, and material circumstances that make them notably different than white student athletes. He writes that " . . . they come from families with lower socioeconomic status . . . have lower entrance scores than white student athletes . . . and report more experiences with racial isolation and discrimination" (79–80). For African American student athletes in predominantly white institutions, academic experiences can heighten feelings of fear.

Like other student athletes with whom I've worked, Tangela worried that instructors might draw her athleticism to the attention of other students. While public acknowledgment may strike instructors as benign, student athletes can experience these remarks as an indictment of their intellectual ability. As Tangela remarked,

> My teacher announced in class, "The women's basketball team has been winning, and we've got an athlete in the class." I didn't want that. I didn't want other students to look at me like that. I didn't want them to be thinking that I was dumb.

Tangela's concern was common among those student athletes I knew and illustrates the delicate nature of live encounters between students and teachers. For some athletes, such attention in classroom settings only reinforced the stigma they associated with their own athleticism. As a tutor in various support programs, I avoided the topic of athletics unless a student athlete was injured or invited such talk. Instead, I spent instructional time assisting students to negotiate their reading, writing, and classroom observations. In the latter case, I often began tutoring sessions by asking students if they were confused about the behavior of teachers or students in any of their classes for the week. Opening minutes of tutoring sessions were thus devoted to interpreting academic "performances" that a student might be struggling to understand.

When students shared concerns about the behavior of their instructors, I tried to present a range of possible interpretations, a means of converting preoccupations with failure to strategic analysis. During the opening weeks of her first semester, for instance, Tangela worried about the response of an instructor from whom she had solicited permission to travel,

> When I went up to my teacher and handed him my travel excuse form, I'm was afraid of how he would react. I was trying to see how he was looking. I know some of them think, "Oh, God, another basketball player. I've got to sign this sheet." Now I'm worrying about how I'm gonna do in that class.

Such fears are common and provide an occasion to talk about how a student might reorient her behavior to signal involvement in the conventional ways that most university instructors understand (sitting near the front of class, notetaking, soliciting individual attention after class, etc.). Such analyses appeal to students like Billy and Nadine, who understood their academic survival in strategic terms. As Nadine asserted, "I try not to be a statistic. Only so many of us [African American student athletes] get through the door. So many of us fall by the wayside. I want to get to the other side. It's like chess, checkers, any game you play. . . . It's a game of life, of survival."

Unlike their male counterparts, female student athletes, regardless of grade point average, were not required to attend the evening and weekend study tables sponsored by the men's athletic department. Instead, a single academic advisor in the women's program assisted participants to locate tutors when the student athletes themselves indicated such arrangements were necessary. As Tangela explained,

> I arrange tutors for my classes during the first couple weeks of school. I know that basketball can be time consuming, and I don't want to get behind in any of my classes. I have to tell my academic advisor what classes that I want tutors for, and she gives me a list of names. I call them and schedule tutoring sessions. There's a penalty if we schedule tutors and don't show up. I always show up for mine.

While Tangela and her teammates were held responsible for tutor contact and appointments, their academic progress did not pass unsupervised. Coaches met on a weekly basis with three to four student athletes for whom they took on the responsibility of academic mentoring, and team practices were held from 5:30–8:30 AM so as not to interrupt the players' academic day. Home and away games were held on Friday nights and Sunday afternoons, which allowed for fewer travel-related class absences. During the two-year period of data collection, I saw no evidence of "clustering" (Lapchick 1989), the practice of enrolling student athletes in only a select group of general education courses.

The female student athletes, their coaches, and a single academic advisor maintained a triadic association that accorded participants considerable authority. All members of the 1995–1996 women's basketball team who remained at Iowa the duration of their careers graduated. Even more impressive, all but two would graduate in just four years. The graduation rate for female intercollegiate student athletes enrolled at the University of Iowa during the 1997–1998 school year was 84.6 percent, a full 21 percent greater than the general student population (Foley and Wirt, 1999, 89). Moreover, the cumulative grade-point average for all female student athletes for spring 1999 was 3.101 (Foley and Wirt, 1999, 89). These figures are well above national averages for female and male intercollegiate student athletes.

By allowing student athletes some governance of their own forms of academic support, the women's athletic department and coaching staff limited redundant retention structures. While there were female participants just as troubled academically as some of their male counterparts, these students had the time and strategic instruction that allowed them not just to acclimate but to take responsibility for their academic learning. The mentoring relationships among female coaches and players were certainly distinct from the variegated and extensive administrative structures that disrupted the live encounters available to male student athletes designated at-risk. For these students, obligatory visits to multiple support programs undermined opportunities for sustained and meaningful interaction across semesters.

The Role of Narrative Reflexivity in Writing Classrooms

Understanding is an event—it is not merely a body of beliefs. . . .
[K]nowledge must be understood in terms of structures of embodied
human understanding, as an interaction of a human . . . with its environment (which includes its language, cultural traditions, values,
institutions, and the history of its social community).

Mark Johnson, *The Body in the Mind* (1987)

A central feature of athletic learning for the Iowa women was the emphasis on understanding as primarily a process. On the court, athletes engendered a "perception-action dialectic" (Crossley, 1996) that was necessarily political, requiring negotiated consensus to arrive at shared meaning. While language, or propositional schemata, assisted learners to characterize their perceptual fields in brief interludes between play, it was the nonverbal codification of embodied mental schemata that was primarily responsible for the reflexive consciousness learners sought during extensive sequences of action. The reflexive circuit (Siegle 1986) from self to other and back to self attuned learners to the significance of process and positionality. Growing familiar with this conceptual orientation at the same time I was teaching freshman composition, I began to consider ways that writing might assist students to bridge thought and action, or more specifically, the physical and the textual. As Nedra Reynolds (1993) suggests, recognizing how language is embodied is necessary if writers are to recognize and take responsibility for their perceptual locations,

> . . . a writer's subject positions are determined by the space of the body, her geographical location, her shifting intellectual positions, her distance or closeness to others, to texts, to events . . . ethos is created when writers locate themselves; it is "a way of claiming and taking responsibility for our positions in the world, for the ways we see, for the places from which we speak." (335–336)

To accept that understanding is a process and that a writer's textual positions are located in concrete activity is to recognize the significant potential of narrative to both document and bridge one's shifting physical, conceptual, and textual positions. The problem, of course, is that an arbitrary distinction between critical knowledge and personal experience can lead to general disregard for the forms and function of narrative. Sidonie Smith (1993) suggests that traditional autobiographical practices have privileged a "narrative itinerary of self-disclosure, retrospective summation, and self-justification" (162). The longstanding notion of narrative as a reflective mode of inquiry overshadows its reflexive potential.

In the mid-1990s, the freshman rhetoric program at the University of Iowa involved a two-semester sequence, the first semester devoted largely to narrative-based writing and speech. For inexperienced instructors, the teaching and evaluation of narrative generated concern. Peers in my advisory group admitted their hesitation, and in some cases resentment, at teaching and assessing personal writing. They recognized the limitations of traditional narrative practices and the problems associated with "possessive individualism" (Shotter 1989), particularly the failure of conventional narratives to welcome new forms and spaces for subjectivity. For many instructors, forms of autobiographical writing existed antithetically to modes of inquiry they understood as critical. As the first semester progressed, it was clear that this discomfort had led some to proceed directly to argumentative assignments more in line with the second semester curriculum. While I sympathized with my teaching peers, I also worried about what the extinction of narrative might mean to students, particularly those inclined to think reflexively. At the same time, I was experimenting with a fall course that incorporated narratives of self and other into a semester-long field project that culminated in an ethnographic essay (Chiseri-Strater and Sunstein 2000). I shared Daniel Mahala and Jody Swilky's (1996) view that

. . . story may be a framework for moving beyond personal narrative. . . . If writers understand how their experience is rooted in various sociohistorical processes and community traditions, they can more
easily move between them, integrating personal and scholarly ways of
knowing the self, others, and the world. (365)

While I regret that I did not have the occasion at Iowa to teach intercollegiate student athletes in entry-level composition courses, I did sense
that those students who were inclined to think reflexively benefited
from narrative-based inquiry that allowed them to reconcile the physical experience of fieldwork and the textual experience of representation.

The field project (see Appendix A) evolved over the course of the
semester and included four stages, each requiring a particular phase of
research and writing. As students drafted each layer of their emerging
project, they had the opportunity to revise preceding subdivisions. Following an introduction to anthropological writing and the concept of
culture, students selected a topic for their semester of inquiry. I encouraged students to research a subculture of personal or professional
interest and to not overlook local subcultures that struck them as marginalized or lacking adequate representation. Once students had identified a topic, I assisted them to develop guiding questions that would
frame the design of their field projects. I encouraged students to understand these guiding questions as an occasion to envision new spaces
for their own subjectivity. In other words, what questions might allow
them to think and learn most deeply through analysis of the perspectives and practices of others? The first stage of the field study, Examining the Self, culminated with an introductory layer of writing in which
students introduced their study, identified their guiding questions, and
accounted for their etic, or outsider, perspective. This account required
a reflective stance, necessitating that students identify how particular
past experiences had shaped the present beliefs they associated with
their subculture (Chiseri-Strater and Sunstein 2000). In this way, students began to understand the ethnographic essay as requiring attention to the social, political, and material influences that situate one's
thinking.

Once students had drafted an initial introductory subdivision that
established their position as outsider, they proceeded to the second
stage of the field project, Entering the Field, a phase that initiated the
gradual shift from reflective to reflexive writing. Students began by
reading and discussing anthropological texts that allowed them to understand how certain textual conventions have traditionally skewed
the representation of others and, at the same time, failed to call the
subjectivity of the researcher into question (Abu-Lughod 1993). Following several field visits and using systematically documented field
notes, students created an "arrival narrative" that conveyed a storied

account of informants' rituals, artifacts, language, and place-making without evacuating the narrative of authorial presence. During this phase, I encouraged students to understand their fieldwork and writing as "performances" for which they must account. According to Elyse Pineau (1994),

> Performance combines full body engagement with critical reflexivity; information must be engaged somatically as well as intellectually. It is the dialectical process of doing and reflecting, experiencing and interpreting that distinguishes performance methodology from simply "acting out." (17)

Writing the arrival narrative represented an opportunity to reconcile bodily and intellectual activity, a stage of writing that inevitably raised questions about the ethics of representation. As Twigg (1994) notes, "the notion of performativity emphasizes the text as more than an activity; it becomes simultaneously a social act and a site where the social is articulated, structured, and struggled over" (2). The emphasis during this unit was narrating one's experiences with others in the larger context of acknowledging the problematics of power, the perspectival influence of informants, and the ethical dimensions of one's inquiry.

In stage three, Interviewing Informants, students relied on their guiding questions and fieldnote data to develop interview questions that would allow informants to account for their own positions in their own language. Here, students considered the dilemmas of ethnographic authority (Clifford 1983) that complicate the representation of others. In some cases, students opted for multiple authorship, granting uninterrupted textual space to the voices of those they interviewed. The result was often a "counter-text" (Shotter 1989) that disrupted the singular authority of the writer and opened the field project to a wider variety of perspectives. Finally in stage four, Coming to Conclusions, students thought inductively, seeking themes that appeared to characterize the perspectives and practices of informants. At this stage, I encouraged students to understand themselves in relation to those they studied. In this way, they completed the reflexive circuit by coming to conclusions not just about others but about their own shifting locations. The final phase of writing required students not just to locate informants' perspectives but to account for how their own location had been shaped by those they studied.

In the fall of 1998, I accepted a senior lecturer position in the department of English at Ohio State University, where I joined other postdoctoral faculty in the undergraduate basic writing program known as The Writing Workshop. The position would allow me to continue refining the ethnographic essay course within a composition program that welcomed reflexive pedagogies (Qualley 1997). At a time when basic writing programs across the country face extinction, The Writing Workshop at Ohio State represents a rare institutional attempt to support the learning of transitional students. During the 1990s, the program consolidated authority for instructing freshmen students who, by virtue of a placement formula, suggested a need for extended instruction in composition. Ideologically, The Writing Workshop exists in contrast to traditional "remediation" programs, which typically operate with little in the way of institutional regard and resources. Housed in a distinct campus location with its own secretarial support and offices, The Writing Workshop exists as a largely autonomous unit. Distinct from the Writing Center, which employs undergraduate and graduate tutors to assist students on a drop-in basis, The Writing Workshop offers a series of basic writing courses for which students receive both credit and a course grade, institutional recognition that lends the program considerable credibility. Much of the success of the basic writing program at Ohio State rests with the kind of ideological orientation that former faculty member Andrea Lunsford (1991) admits poses challenges to any institution,

> The idea of a center informed by a theory of knowledge as socially constructed, of power and control as constantly negotiated and shared, and of collaboration as its first principle presents quite a challenge. It challenges our ways of organizing our centers, of training our staff . . . and of working with teachers. It even challenges our sense of where we "fit" in this idea. More importantly, however, such a center presents a challenge to the institution of higher education, an institution that insists on rigidly controlled individual performance, on evaluation as punishment, on isolation. . . . (9)

Across courses in the program students received supplementary instruction from peer tutors and graduate extended instructor tutors who attended their classes. Multiple layers of support within a single transitional program allowed students to understand their teachers and tutors as connected members of an intelligible program.

Instructors in The Writing Workshop met on a weekly basis to consider, refine, and implement pedagogical practices that fostered the dialectical engagement of their students. Across courses, faculty incorporated a host of practices that observed the link between concrete experience and abstract thought. These included portfolios, computer-mediated authoring and communication, oral histories, apprenticeships, problem-based inquiry service learning, and fieldwork. To the extent that courses in The Writing Workshop supported the integration of services and the involvement of students in their own learning, they resembled what Jean Lave and Etienne Wenger (1991) describe as "communities of practice." The central feature of such groups is the participatory engagement of members. As Lave and Wenger write,

> Participation is always based on situated negotiation and renegotiation of meaning in the world. This implies that understanding and experience are in constant interaction—indeed are mutually constitutive. The notion of participation thus dissolves dichotomies between cerebral and embodied activity, between contemplation and involvement, between abstraction and experience: persons, actions, and the world are implicated in all thought, speech, knowing, and learning. (51–62)

Reorienting spatial and interactional features, Writing Workshop teachers and students engaged in practices that foregrounded dialectical engagement not just with each other but with resources beyond the classroom. Such pedagogies, supported by peer groups and extended instruction tutors, also allowed for considerable peer response, editing, and revision, the kind of process-oriented practices that encouraged students to perceive their writing and thinking through the perspectives of readers.

The Writing Workshop is one of few basic writing programs in the country that has survived and prospered in ways that affect the retention of those who make knowledge in diverse ways. For several reasons, the program is promising. First, it serves transitional students on their entrance to the university, a time when they are most inclined to struggle with the sensibility of an institution that so often splinters their identity. Second, basic writing faculty are skilled in reflexive pedagogies that respond to the full range of conceptual diversity. Course enrollments limited to 15 students are taught in classrooms that allow for circular seating, an arrangement that invites students and their instructor to maintain visual access to each other during discussions. On the perimeter of the classrooms, individual stations allow for computer-mediated instruction. In this way, oral and written language is an outgrowth of embodied action via direct and technological interactions. Two significant weaknesses limit the influence of The Writing Workshop. First, its faculty do not receive salaries and benefits commensurate with their educational rank and expertise. Second, the program exists in conjunction with parallel support programs across the university, thus contributing to redundant layers of academic "support."

Understanding their voices as located in experiential contexts and live encounters, writers can rely on narrative as a reflexive opportunity to negotiate the often dichotomized conditions of mind and body, self and other. Narrative reflexivity recognizes the experience of border crossing (Giroux 1993) and perceptual negotiation (Horner and Lu 2000) without disassociating these struggles from concrete relations and activities. Political and ethical issues associated with representation are not abstract concepts but are connected directly to one's physical and social location in and across communities. Put simply, one's embodied activity is the *means* to language and thought.

Flawed Reform: The Problematic Reliance on NCAA Initiatives

Aside from the absence of live encounters in the academic domain, perhaps the greatest impediment to athletic and academic reform has been the ongoing reliance on National Collegiate Athletic Association (NCAA) mandates. To illustrate the problematic nature of institutional reform, I return to the late 1980s, a turbulent period for administrators, coaches, and faculty at the University of Iowa. During this period, various significant violations were uncovered in the Hawkeye football program. In a 1989 federal trial of Chicago sports agent Norby Walters, former football players Ronnie Harmon and Devon Mitchell admitted that they had received illegal payments from Walters during their college years. As word of the Harmon and Mitchell scandal broke, state newspapers also disclosed that academic transcripts for the two included courses in billiards, bowling, military organization, and watercolor painting. In the wake of publicized problems, former University of Iowa president Hunter Rawlings assigned law professor David Vernon to chair an in-house investigation of the athletic department and its programming.

Across NCAA Division I universities nationwide, cases of impropriety during the late 1980s received widespread publicity. In 1987, a faculty committee at Auburn University found quarterback Jeff Berger guilty of plagiarism and recommended suspension, a decision later overturned by the vice-president of academic affairs. In breach of contract suits brought separately against Creighton University and the Board of Trustees of the California State Universities and Colleges, intercollegiate student athletes alleged a host of illegalities, including denial of sufficient counseling, pressure to enroll in certain courses to preserve eligibility, denial of access to remedial courses, and transcript violations. Both suits were settled out of court. During the 1988–1989 school year, various football players at the University of Oklahoma were charged with attempted murder, rape, and distribution of controlled substances, what interim president David Swan termed "isolated incidents" (qtd. in Funk 1991, 97). In 1991, the Ohio State University's touted tailback Robert Smith, a sophomore pre-medicine student, quit the football team citing frequent pressure he received from coaching staff to miss class in order to attend football practices or team meetings.

During the early 1990s, President Rawlings, a member of the NCAA Presidents Commission, urged the supervisory body to tighten national eligibility requirements, namely to ban freshmen from varsity competition. Rawlings' recommendation reoriented the debate among NCAA delegates, for whom initial eligibility legislation seemed to be a predominant focus. In 1986, the NCAA had proposed Proposition 48, which required prospective intercollegiate athletes to maintain a 2.0 grade-point average in core courses in high school and to score above 700 (out of 1600) on the SAT, or 15 (out of 36) on the composite ACT. During its first year in effect, the percentage of African American freshmen on Division I intercollegiate teams fell 18 percent while the percentage of white freshmen increased slightly (Suggs 1999a, A48).

At the NCAA convention in January 1991, the Presidents Commission again considered the possibility of tighter initial eligibility requirements. Meanwhile, on his own campus, Rawlings urged the approval of a freshmen nonparticipation policy, a campaign that elicited defiant response from athletic officials and a general public who maintained that legislating isolated institutional change would undermine recruitment.

In 1992, delegates to the NCAA convention passed Proposition 16, which would take effect in 1996. The legislation further increased initial eligibility requirements. Under Proposition 16, prospective student athletes would now be expected to score at a certain level on the SAT or ACT, as well as earn a certain grade-point average in 13 core courses in high school. According to the Prop 16 qualifier index, for example, an athlete with a grade-point average of 2.5 would be required to score 820 on the SAT while a player with a grade-point average of 2.0 would be required to score 1,010 on the SAT (Bassinger 1997, A48). The legislation also allowed for partial qualifier status for freshmen who fell just below requirements.

With the passage of Proposition 16, members of the Black Coaches Association (BCA) waged an informational campaign that highlighted the racial inequities reproduced by eligibility guidelines that privileged standardized assessments like the SAT and ACT. As president of the BCA, Rudy Washington, a former Iowa assistant men's basketball coach and then head coach of men's basketball at Drake University in Des Moines, Iowa, enlisted the support of C. Vivian Stringer, then head women's basketball coach in Iowa City. During the 1994–1995 basketball season, a prominent national coalition of African American coaches, including Stringer, threatened a coaching boycott to publicize their concerns. The potential disruption prompted inflammatory public response, particularly in Iowa, where a lack of racial diversity in conjunction with no existing state mandates for elementary and secondary student assessment afforded the public little context for understanding race issues at the heart of the NCAA-BCA standoff. The University of Iowa seemed a microcosm of the national debate. Responding to improprieties, university administrators considered reforms that disturbed coaches, some of whom held convictions about the decline of educational opportunities for African American students. Response from the public, largely critical of any change, further complicated discussions of reform.

Nearly a decade after the passage of Proposition 16, the NCAA faces a legal bind. In January 1997, a lawsuit challenging its constitutionality was filed in U.S. District Court in Philadelphia. On behalf of four former high school athletes, the lawsuit alleged that the qualifier index mandated by Proposition 16 unfairly emphasizes standardized test scores. According to Trial Lawyers for Public Justice, the organization representing the plaintiffs, the use of standardized test scores to establish initial eligibility was "determined, implemented, and enforced by the NCAA without proper validation studies and with disregard for the unjustifiable disparate impact that the minimum test score requirement would have on African-American student athletes" (qtd. in Haworth 1997, 1). On March 8, 1999, a federal judge ruled that the standardized test scores composing the NCAA qualifier index discriminated against African American athletes and thus violated Title VI of the Civil Rights Act of 1964 (Suggs 1999b, A56). Filing a hasty appeal in late March 1999, the NCAA received a stay of execution from a three-judge panel of the U.S. Court of Appeals for the Third Circuit. Until a decision on the appeal is announced, the NCAA has notified all delegates and participating institutions that Proposition 16 remains in effect.

The question of constitutionality is only one reason to question continued reliance on NCAA directives. Disturbing, as well, is the fact that the national clearinghouse responsible for processing prospective student athletes' applications for eligibility is operated by American College Testing, producer of one of the two standardized tests mandated by Proposition 16 legislation. The arrangement is one of many reasons critics characterize the NCAA as primarily an economic cartel.[1] Until a body with no commercial investment in standardized assessment oversees the NCAA clearinghouse, there exists considerable reason to scrutinize legislation that further increases the emphasis placed on testing in the eligibility process. Ultimately, my work with student athletes led me to understand how NCAA policies have *not* encouraged university administrators and faculty to reform academic practices, programming, and policies. What remained the most formidable barrier for the student athletes with whom I've worked was not eligibility requirements but the lack of sustained and strategic instruction that fostered their sense of academic involvement.

The Limitations of Initial Eligibility Legislation

Around the time of the BCA campaign, I began work with an African American junior college transfer student I will call Anthony. Recruited to fill a sudden vacancy on an Iowa athletic team, Anthony accepted an opportunity not available to him as a prospective freshman when he

had failed to meet Proposition 48 standards. A "Prop 48 casualty," he
had entered a junior college system that operated beyond NCAA juris-
diction. I recall Anthony because he is a reminder that the incredible
energy academic and athletic administrators invest debating initial eligibility requirements does not directly influence the endless migration
of junior college transfers, those who are often too troubled academically to succeed at public universities but receive admittance anyway.
Anthony should never have been admitted to the University of Iowa.
While he was an unusual case, the only transfer student I tutored during my decade of employment in the Office of Student Services, Anthony represented a varying but serious problem across public universities nationwide.

By the time he arrived at Iowa, Anthony's post-secondary education had been transitory. As a freshman, he had attended a junior college in California. As a sophomore, he had moved to a junior college in
the Midwest. From there, he caught the eye of Iowa recruiters who required depth at his position. As a junior, Anthony transferred again,
this time to the University of Iowa. In August, an athletic advisor in the
Office of Student Services phoned me the first week of the semester.
Anthony was already an academic concern and would require much
time and support. I wasn't sure I could manage the commitment, particularly when initial reports of Anthony's writing and reading abilities
seemed to suggest that his academic record at two junior colleges might
possibly have been inflated. In my initial meeting with Anthony, I
asked him to talk about the kind of tutorial support that would be most
helpful to him. Straightening in his chair, Anthony sat as if at any second he might dart from the room. His left hand gripped one armrest
and his right seized the strap of a burgundy backpack so that only a
corner of its base rested on the floor. Before I could rephrase my question, I made the mistake of sinking heavily into my swivel chair, a motion that always triggered its aging spring mechanism to slip, hurling
me backward, a catapult gone berserk. Had it not been for my arms and
the wide, looping strokes of a hasty mid-air butterfly, I might have found
myself in an unseemly reverse somersault. As it was, I still looked the
fool, but I had fought gravity and won. And I had made Anthony laugh.

Anthony and I met almost daily for a year and a half. That first
year, Anthony's eagerness to schedule additional tutoring appointments made it hard to set time limits on our tutorials. Anthony was
learning a great deal, but his disadvantages and needs were so immense
that I sensed he would never alter the realities of his educational history. Whenever Anthony faced a writing assignment, we approached it
orally, first reading the assignment as it was presented. After isolating
relevant details, we would brainstorm possible organizational formats.
Throughout the process, I introduced Anthony not just to the conven-

tions of academic prose but to the implicit rationale that grounded such conventions. Like all students, Anthony required a strategic understanding of the purposes of and expectations for academic writing. Anthony composed in a series of stages that began with oral composition. As Anthony responded to particular points of the assignment, I recorded his talk in writing. I provided Anthony a transcript of his talk, a script that became the basis for distinguishing vernacular and standard language forms. This process from oral to written text constituted Anthony's first success at writing.

Anthony's struggle to read and compose seemed to have resulted from a history of profound educational inequity, desperate family circumstances, learning disabilities that were later diagnosed, and paralyzing self-doubt. In my mind, Anthony represented the most troubling dimension of intercollegiate athletics. Traversing from one college to the next in order to sidestep initial NCAA eligibility legislation, Anthony had never been expected to learn. As he admitted to me, tutors in the junior colleges he attended had written papers on his behalf and, in lecture hall test situations, test-takers had been arranged. On his entrance to the University of Iowa, Anthony had asked athletic officials to be red-shirted, a request that would allow him a year to focus on his studies without being required to play and without losing eligibility. Like all junior college transfers, Anthony had been recruited to fill an immediate vacancy. He was not granted the opportunity accorded some freshmen student athletes with marginal academic status. Anthony had to play. And concurrently, Anthony had to learn to write. I knew that a diploma from the university was unlikely. Still, the transfer of grades from Anthony's junior college transcript, albeit grades that were questionable in their own right, would offset low marks Anthony received at Iowa. In all ways, the situation was disturbing.

By continuing to work with Anthony, I realize I may well have sustained a long history of educational abuse. Nevertheless, I did so not because I felt altering Anthony's past or future education was possible but because I wanted to assist him as long as he desired to learn. This was also the sentiment I made clear to Anthony. Whatever unfolded in the course of time could not be allowed to preempt his momentary successes. As long as Anthony possessed an opportunity and a desire to learn, I would assist him. Certainly, Anthony understood how choices he had made in junior college had sabotaged his learning, but he also blamed educational institutions that had failed him. From grade school through junior college, he acknowledged that the only expectations held for him were that he attend class. In light of such little support, it's not surprising that this became the only expectation Anthony held for himself. As I suspected, Anthony did not fulfill his academic requirements by the end of his two-year scholarship. Though the men's athletic department did agree to fund an additional semester, Anthony's junior college grades no longer mediated his low grades at Iowa. Like Billy, he withdrew.

The Threat of Academic Fraud

My work with Anthony acquainted me with the fine line between academic support and fraud. Had several layers of academic support not been available, I suspect Anthony might never have been admitted to the university. Instead, these programs became the rationale by which athletic and academic staff justified his admittance. That I was involved in an academic struggle I suspected would result in failure is only one step from actually manipulating the learning of students like Anthony so they do not fail.

Outright cases of academic fraud have led many to question the role of academic retention programs housed in athletic departments. In March 1999, in St. Paul, Minnesota, *The Pioneer Press* reported that Jan Gangelhoff, a former office manager in the academic counseling office in the University of Minnesota men's athletic department, had written over 400 assignments that student athletes had submitted to professors as their own (Dohrmann 1999). Upset at how she had been phased out of her association with the men's basketball program, Gangelhoff had contacted the newspaper, providing reporters with samples of the course work she had written. Gangelhoff acknowledged receiving cash payments for her services from Clem Haskins, head men's basketball coach. About the actual process of composing Gangelhoff explained,

> It depended on what we needed to do. If it was a homework assignment and they [the students] had been to class, we would talk about what happened in class and what they heard and what they thought about the assignment. And then they would take the remote and go watch TV, and I would type the assignment up. (qtd. in Dohrmann 1999, A1)

In most NCAA Division I institutions, athletic departments house their own academic retention programs, relying on a pool of many dozens of content area tutors, who are supervised, in turn, by a corps of athletic academic advisors. The improprieties at Minnesota indicate how readily instructional staff employed by athletic departments can undermine the learning of student athletes.

In my own experience as a retention tutor, I found my supervisors, the academic advisors, nearly paralyzed by responsibilities to both athletic and academic branches of the university. I often wondered what degree of joy they could derive from responsibilities that seemed to please neither coaches, student athletes, nor faculty. Gary Funk (1991), an athletic academic advisor at Southwest Missouri State University writes that such individuals "are often caught in a no man's land between the academic and the athletic—not jock enough or coach enough to have real power in the athletic department and viewed with suspicion by the faculty as someone tainted by the athletic monster" (126–127). For all the reasons that academic programming has fragmented and specialized, athletic departments, too, have grown complex. The athletic academic advisor came into being as athletic programs expanded and began to recruit students who required academic support (Funk 1991). As liaisons between the athletic and academic realms, these staff members monitor all facets of the retention program, including supervision of tutors, written documentation of each student athlete's academic progress, operation of study tables, correspondence with faculty instructors, and so on. Responsible for hundreds of student athletes, each enrolled in four to six classes, overworked athletic academic advisors often have little opportunity to scrutinize the quality of tutorial instruction.

While structures and policies within athletic departments may complicate the work of athletic advisors, they are often key supports in the lives of student athletes. These advisors represent a critical link between the realms of sport and school. Because student athletes face distinct conceptual dilemmas, this constituency requires advising attuned to the realities of athletic and academic learning. Administrative reshuffling that places advising responsibilities in the hands of general college personnel unfamiliar with or unsympathetic toward intercollegiate student athletes poses considerable risk to retention. My own experience with academic athletic advisors suggests their jobs demanded a sensitivity to racial and class dilemmas that advisors in the general colleges of predominantly white universities may have little consistent occasion to experience. Given that some student athletes feel considerable degrees of fear and alienation toward their academic involvement, advisors must be skilled at recognizing how apprehension and resistance intersect.

In the wake of the Minnesota scandal, Mark G. Yudof, the university's president, initiated institutional restructuring that shifted responsibilities for academic advising and retention of student athletes to the provost's office. The reform is similar to the one in place at the University of Virginia for nearly five years (Suggs 1999c, A51). While it's too early to assess the merit of such transfers of authority, my sense is that in and of themselves they represent quick and public fixes more attuned to crises of institutional identity than to crises of student attrition. Shifting funding sources and office locations does not necessarily make the university any more sensible and less threatening to student athletes. For this reason, transfers of authority should be considered the first step in a more comprehensive attempt to integrate and improve the academic support universities make available to all students. In the event these transfers occur without concern for the training of instructors and advisors, they remain political gestures oriented toward the restoration of public confidence.

Confronting the Issue of Academic Integrity

When I encounter sweeping attacks on student athletes or cries of academic decline as a result of their presence, I keep in mind a still timely *Harvard Educational Review* article in which David Cohen (1976) suggests that social policy in education has long reflected two conflicting responses to modernity. One response manifests itself in the rhetoric of loss, relying on appeals to declining standards, moral decay, and social and personal disintegration. In April 1998, the Rutgers 1000 campaign, sponsored by a coalition of faculty, alumni, and students, escalated its drive to "halt the decline of academic and intellectual standards at Rutgers University." Holding its central administration and athletic program responsible for fiscal and intellectual drain, Rutgers 1000 proponents enticed 1932 alumnus and Nobel Prize economist Milton Friedman to respond. Of the university's mission, Friedman announced, "Universities exist to transmit knowledge and understanding of ideas and values to students, not to provide entertainment for spectators or employment for athletes" (qtd in "A Brief Guide" 1999, 2). Such a remark demands scrutiny. To claim the relationship between universities and those to whom they provide athletic scholarships is flatly contractual is to deny the educational convictions of most student athletes. Further, to argue that postsecondary institutions "exist to transmit knowledge" rejects outright the transactional nature of critical inquiry. It may be that administrators, faculty, and public officials who espouse transmissive pedagogies are less inclined to recognize the bodily and conceptual orientations of others. I suspect that the lack of schematic portability the Iowa women experienced across contexts of their athletic and academic learning posed conceptual dilemmas that may well characterize the struggles of nonscholarship students acculturated to think in diverse ways. The reliance on transmissive pedagogies may serve a gatekeeping role that restricts the range of conceptual diversity represented in public institutions.

As David Cohen (1976) argues, the drive to preserve an institutional pastlife is only one response to modernity. The other is to enter into social policy questions with a sense of invention. Enacting this latter perspective, Annette Kolodny (1998) has written of administrative dilemmas she faced during her five years as dean of humanities at the University of Arizona. She addresses the serious fiscal and logistical problems that now accompany demographic changes in the student bodies of most public universities. Interestingly, Kolodny's policy recommendations do not include excising student athletes or athletic programs from university life. Resisting the rhetoric of loss, Kolodny addresses serious institutional problems encouraging "a language of schooling that honors difference, diversity, risk-taking, imagination, and social responsibility" (256).

Kolodny's and Friedman's perspectives represent diametric responses to institutional policy and mission. With respect to intercollegiate sport, these perspectives play out in two ways. Either student athletes and intercollegiate sport are deemed irredeemable threats to intellectual inquiry and thereby eliminated or curtailed, or—as I recommend—they are understood as central to the broader imperatives enacted on behalf of student diversity. This latter perspective welcomes modernity with attention to how institutional structures, policies, and pedagogies jeopardize educational access for students whose embodied histories as learners do not dovetail with tradition.

Until public institutions invest materially in an ideological shift that reconciles mind and body, individuals who employ reflexive pedagogies will continue to be dismissed as "soft," "service-oriented," or even "superficial." To initiate institutional reforms at the University of Arizona, Annette Kolodny increased the material resources available to faculty interested in, and intellectually inclined to support, the development of embodied teaching practices. Grants were allocated to faculty who expanded and refined their understanding of what it means to teach to students who make knowledge in diverse ways. As Kolodny explains,

> Clearly, there is no lack of good intentions. What is lacking is any systematic attentiveness, across the disciplines and across the nation's campuses, to the very fact of cognitive diversity. That lack of attentiveness makes progress slow and piecemeal. Faculty members ready to begin the pedagogical and curricular retooling that I am recommending here require incentives and support. . . . As always during my years as dean, I began with incentives. (1998, 168–169)

Concern for embodied cognition begins with scrutiny of the ideological divide between mind and body that infiltrates every dimension of university life. Such concern requires us to recognize the conceptual significance of the human body and to analyze how institutional life disembodies teaching and learning at considerable emotional and intellectual cost to those who already feel powerless.

Recommendations for Reform

Nearly a decade after the passage of Proposition 16, the constitutionality of initial eligibility legislation is in question. While NCAA subcommittees continue to discuss and formulate other remedies to attrition, there exists little indication that the supervisory body will approve radical directives. Recently, the National Alliance for College Athletic Reform, a grassroots organization composed of faculty, administrators, and public officials, has charged that intercollegiate athletic programs are responsible for undermining the academic missions of midsize and large public universities. After two meetings, NAFCAR has issued five recommendations for reform. In part, the group urges the public disclosure of academic records for all intercollegiate student athletes. Their proposal recommends that

> . . . universities publicly disclose the academic major, academic adviser, courses listed by academic major, general education requirements, and electives, including course GPA and instructor for all students. No individual's grades will be disclosed. . . . The university will disclose for each intercollegiate athletic team the courses enrolled in by team members, the average of the grades given in the course, and instructor of the course at the end of the semester. (NAFCAR 2000, 1)

With little regard for the Family Educational Right to Privacy Act, NAFCAR recommendations risk violating the federally protected privacy rights of all university students. In their aggressive mistrust of athletic staff, coaches, and student athletes, NAFCAR members seem willing to deny constitutional rights that their respective institutions must honor in order to retain federal funding. More importantly, the targeted criticism of athletic programs and student athletes allows NAFCAR officials the luxury of ignoring the mitigating effects of academic programs, policies, and pedagogies.

The most promising avenue of reform remains the volitional action of athletic conference officials, university presidents, and academic councils. Institutional committees investigating the academic integration and welfare of student athletes must be capable of sidestepping seductive and grand rhetorical arguments that posit blame. Initiatives should reward tenured faculty who model reflexive pedagogies in entry-level composition and general education courses. Above all, revising athletic and academic structures must begin with an appreciation for the ideological divide that can undermine student athletes' connection to nonscholarship students and to academic life. While ideological and economic features shaping the women's athletic administration at Iowa insured the academic support of coaches, such mentoring is rare. Ultimately, reformers must consider how support services housed in the academic realm can assist student athletes to establish and maintain interaction with nonscholarship students and faculty. To this end, the following changes would be beneficial:

- Implement a practice but nonparticipation rule for scholarship athletes in those intercollegiate sports that do not meet a standard measure of academic progress.

- Solicit the participation of student athletes from high-revenue sports on all advisory committees investigating academic and athletic reform.

- Eliminate all course sections that fail to integrate student athletes with nonscholarship students.

- Transfer athletic academic advisors to funding lines and offices located in the general college. Advisors making a shift from athletic to academic affiliation should retain their caseloads *until* academic advisors who agree to mentor student athletes have received training that sensitizes them to the distinct demands and dilemmas that shape student athletes' learning.

- Eliminate academic support services (bookstores, libraries, tutorial services) housed in athletic departments. Integrate tutorial staff into existing programs in the general college.

- Eliminate redundant academic support structures that serve mainly to employ and train tutors, to advance the service and scholarship agendas of faculty, and/or to elevate the material and political interests of select departments or colleges.

- Restrict staffing in basic writing programs to nontenure stream faculty. Graduate instructors should not be responsible for these programs. Under the direction of a tenure stream director of freshman composition, such programs should be housed in proximity to freshman counseling, advising, and tutorial staffs. Classroom time should include regular and uninterrupted use of computer technologies. Additional funding for salaries, benefits, and material resources might come from the redirection of coaches' income currently garnered from athletic shoe, clothing, and equipment endorsements to the general college. For many student athletes, the direction of endorsement stipends to head coaches is often a source of considerable resentment.

- Develop institutional and interinstitutional grants for faculty interested in designing entry-level composition and general education courses attuned to conceptual diversity. These courses should highlight bodily engagement as a means to particular disciplinary discourses. As Robert and Michele Root-Bernstein suggest, " . . . first, provide [students] with a rich repertoire of creative mental tools, such as imaging, abstracting, empathizing or play-acting, kinesthetic thinking, analogizing, and modeling; and second, train them in the skills needed to translate what they learn through these tools into formal, symbolic languages" (2000, A64).

- In the development of nontenure stream appointments, consult the Conference on College Composition and Communication Task Force for Improving the Working Conditions of Part-Time and Adjunct Faculty.

- Adopt the Southeastern Conference proposal that would accord athletic scholarships to athletic teams based on the graduation rates of their respective student athletes. The proposal dictates that for each player who fails to graduate, a reduction of one scholarship would exist through what would have been the remainder of that student's athletic participation. Under this proposal, students in poor academic standing cannot receive an athletic scholarship from another institution, though no penalty is directed toward a program from which an athlete leaves for professional participation.

Notes

1. James Koch (1994) is one of many who have challenged the viability of the National Collegiate Athletic Association. According to Koch, "The NCAA is a cartel because it: (a) sets the maximum price that can be paid for intercollegiate athletes; (b) regulates the quantity of athletes that can be purchased in a given time period; (c) regulates the duration and intensity of usage of those athletes; (d) on occasion fixes the price at which sports outputs can be sold; (e) purports to control the property rights to activities such as . . . televising . . . ; (f) periodically informs cartel members about transactions, costs, market conditions, and sales techniques; (g) occasionally pools and distributes portions of the cartel's profits; and (h) polices the behavior of its members and levies penalties against those . . . who are deemed in violation of cartel rules and regulations" (136).

Chapter Five

Minding the Body

In May 1997, as my thesis deadline approached, I continued to assist members of the women's basketball team who were in need of transportation, a place to study, a meal, or advice on assignments. And they continued to help me, approving chapter drafts, recommending changes, or running campus errands. Despite the reciprocity, I felt increasingly overwhelmed. During the course of the second season, my contact with players had increased, even though I no longer attended morning practices. In the spring I began to feel frustrated, angry even, at situations that forced me to delay my own academic obligations. Though I did not pull out of relationships, I had begun to resent interruptions that impeded my writing.

One afternoon, prior to a tutoring session at her apartment, Simone asked, as always, if I had eaten. Usually, I respected how little food players could afford to buy and how much they required for their own sustenance. For lunch, Simone wanted to share a favorite Jamaican recipe that included ackee fruit, dried cod, and dumplings. With the mention of dried cod, my thoughts raced. As a child, my Yuletide spirit had nosedived with each approaching Sons of Norway lutefisk dinner, an evening when a single church basement became a virtual Valhalla for an ethnic community that viewed the annual arrival of Norwegian cod, dried and preserved in lye, as cause for celebration. Boiled with potatoes and served with lefse, the lutefisk was an olfactory nightmare that became acutely real once it hit the palate. For my brother and me, those Scandinavian dinners induced severe paroxysms, wretching and writhings that to our dismay never summoned an ounce of parental remorse.

With brisk swipes of a knife, Simone explained her recipe to the bob and boil of salted cod and dumplings in a worn red pot. The vibrant yellow ackee, a fruit sent to her canned from Jamaica, elicited a stream of stories. As she chopped, Simone spoke of how, as a child, she and other children in the neighborhood would often contribute to a meal. One child sharing a family pot, others picking the ackee, still others providing cod or dumplings. As I listened to Simone, I realized that her dried cod had sustained Jamaicans just as lutefish had sustained my ancestors, Norwegians who gauged the depth of their winters by looking to the frozen ports along the Boknafjorden for signs of spring. Simone's knowledge, emotion, and memory of Jamaica, embodied in this single culinary ritual she had chosen to share with me, underscored all that I had learned during the course of my study. In the reflexive way that her teammates had lived and learned, I saw through Simone's history to my own.

For the first time in weeks, I was no longer resentful. Of all things, I began to think about dried cod and how, in my own ethnic experience, the ceremonial preparation of lutefisk was a collective performance that had allowed a small Midwestern community to remember its past and itself. For the first time, I understood the powerful irony that such communality should survive within an overarching culture that rewarded competition. I was suddenly interested in lutefisk and emailed my mother for information on those who were now preparing the Scandinavian dinners I had attended as a child. Matter of factly, she replied, "I think as the Norwegian ladies who prepared the fish died off, the dinners died, too. They may still do something. Swedish meatballs perhaps, but the lutefisk is gone."

I began to understand both the power and fragility of cultural spaces that foster the interdependence of body and mind. And I understood the source of my resentment. Having returned in the spring to the solitary endeavor that is academic writing, I had resumed a bodily and conceptual orientation distinct from the one I had minded during fieldwork. Because I did not cease contact with informants, I remained the beneficiary and provider of support that these relationships required. What I resented was the oscillation between forms of bodily and conceptual activity that the student athletes themselves negotiated on a daily basis. Across the contexts of their learning, these students shifted from an intermental experience of body and mind that demanded negotiated perception to an intramental experience of mind that often necessitated the denial of body and collectivity.

For players in this study, the shared experience of time, space, and activity supported the emergence, rehearsal, and negotiation of embodied mental structures. Referential to others, the character and constitution of players' knowledge was intersubjective, a form of reflexivity distinct from metamention (Bogdan 2000), which involves the internal, hermeneutical encounter between self and idea. What may distinguish intersubjectivity from metamention, or self-reflexivity, is the powerful experience of affect and the dynamic tension that live encounters can introduce. That coaches and players sustained their encounters off the court was due in part to a streamlined women's athletic administration that necessitated the involvement and academic mentoring of coaches and a single advisor. The context was one that assisted learners to reconcile athletic and academic roles and responsibilities.

During the last two decades I have benefited from sociocognitive (Bruner 1978; Gardner 1983; Vygotsky 1986) and sociocultural (Bakhtin 1981; Volosinov 1986) theories of language and learning that have explained how individuals and groups, located culturally, make knowledge. In her landmark ethnography *Ways with Words*, Shirley Brice Heath (1984) documented multiple contexts of language use, noting distinct and consequential cultural disjunctures. In the mid-eighties, Frederick Erickson (1988) wrote,

> All literacies . . . are radically constituted by their contexts of use. . . .
> Change the physical form of the tools or symbols, or change the social
> form of relations among the people with whom the individual is
> learning . . . and one has profoundly changed the nature of . . . the
> learning. (205)

While constructivist approaches have been central to my professional development, I recognize, too, that their focus upon the conceptual significance of language has not squarely challenged a longstanding devaluation of the human body. From culture to body to mind, I have traced the emergence of embodied schemata responsible for participants' experiences of knowing as athletes. In doing so, I have been attentive to how the human body can enhance the connection between activity and thought. Embodied mental structures are neither preverbal nor preliterate. Although they are distinct from those propositional structures that guide language and other symbolic forms, they are no less significant to learning.

In his ethnographic investigation of learning in a private Canadian high school, Peter McLaren (1993) documented various "states of interaction," what I would argue are distinct patterns of bodily activity that hold conceptual significance. McLaren noted the effect of transmissive classroom practices upon students' experience of self, other, and knowledge. While he did not consider the connection of bodily activity to schemata, McLaren does identify a dilemma that this study bears out. He writes,

> The pretense that learning is primarily a product of individual student
> volition . . . inured the students to the absence of real, active, participatory experience. Students were reduced to the role of pure spectators who assimilated knowledge about things rather than knowledge
> of things in relation to other things. (1993, 119)

Much like the students in McLaren's study, members of the women's basketball team acknowledged the conceptual struggle they encountered when learning necessitated an isolated, nonrelational experience of body. Disembodied learning impinged upon their capacity to establish relations with others, to experience affect and agency, and to know in any creative and critical way.

Prior to my working relationship with Tangela, I had assumed that across the context of their university learning, female athletes probably experienced less conceptual distress than their male counterparts. The longer I had worked with intercollegiate student athletes who participated in football, the more worried I grew about the excessive acculturation to force schemata required of these young men. Many had already spent their entire lives in communities that had led them to acculturate to and agonize about the imposition of concrete and abstract forces, both upon themselves and their families. When I remember Billy, I remember a young man who held deep convictions about what he wished to achieve as a university student. And I think of a young man who possessed the academic abilities necessary to acquire the diploma he envisioned. What happened to Billy was what I had witnessed in others. A mind–body split internalized as a consequence of material inequity long before he came to the university converged with an ideological divide embodied in the very structure of the institution he attended. The lack of integration across academic and athletic domains only reinforced Billy's conceptual sense that he was an object of forces he felt powerless to redirect.

Performing in two university-mandated yet disparate domains, many student athletes are taught to think about and experience their bodies in strict material terms. In high-profile sports like football and basketball, which rely upon embodied schemata increasingly oriented toward force, student athletes may lack access to collaborative relationships that assist them to understand the ideological rift between academic and athletic domains. Certainly, the large number of players required to sustain an intercollegiate football team through a season creates a dangerous anonymity for players. In a context in which only the fittest members play, those who succumb to injury are quickly forgotten. About football, sports journalist Mariah Burton Nelson (1994) writes,

> Commentators' synonyms for "tackled" include hit, drilled, buried, upended, attacked, pounded, gang tackled, sacked, wrapped up, put down on one's face, hammered down, knocked down, ridden down, wrestled down, and hunted down. Former Oakland Raiders coach John Madden has commented, "When something bad happens to you, you don't let it bother you. You do something bad to the other guys." (202)

The relationship of those who possess abstract power and those who exert it concretely is further exacerbated by a hierarchical team structure in which three or four players vie for single offensive and defensive starting positions. Ultimately, the mind–body dichotomy enforced by some coaches and faculty only complicates student athletes' sense of connection to academic life. The splintered nature of their lives contributes to their alienation from nonscholarship students and from an academic realm that is often interpreted for them by coaches, athletic support staff, and upperclassmen.

What surprised me during the investigation of female student athletes was the extent to which they, too, felt stigmatized by their athleticism. As athletes, they not only failed to comply with expectations for feminine comportment but they worried that their athleticism would lead teachers and peers to understand them as physically gifted but intellectually insignificant. Only in their athletic learning did they reconcile the dichotomy of mind and body that was so troublesome to them in other cultural spaces. Coaches and players in this study understood their court learning as embodied, a process I document in terms of intersecting and expanding particulars of place, activity, and mind. Recurrent patterns of time, space, and motion, rehearsed and refined each practice, fostered image schemata that, in turn, guided participants' concrete and abstract thought.

Players cultivated relational knowing on court through bodily orientation toward systemic balance. To achieve concrete and conceptual balance, participants accepted their place in a network of coparticipatory yet asymmetric relations. The balance schema that characterized participants' learning in this context was reinforced by an institutional structure that allowed for intimate relationships among support staff, coaches, and players.

Certainly, the increasing material significance of women's professional basketball raises the possibility that it may be too late for women to retain this transgressive and transformative context of learning. In the same way that men's athletic departments in public universities have invested financially in hierarchical and compartmentalized administrative structures, women's intercollegiate programs are appearing to follow. I suspect that the rising professionalization of women's intercollegiate basketball will lead to fragmented athletic structures and experiences for female players as well. At the University of Tennessee, for instance, Pat Summitt, the women's head basketball coach, has reportedly made extensive physical screening a component of her recruiting program. In at least one instance, a student athlete recruited by the Lady Volunteers was eliminated from consideration when medical screening procedures suggested she *might* be at risk of future knee injury (qtd. in Mc-Callum 1995). Such a policy, common in men's intercollegiate athletics, intensifies student athletes' belief that they are valued only for their physical potential.

During fieldwork, as I read across disciplines in the humanities and social sciences, I found that theories of embodiment tended to emphasize the relation of the social body and the individual, accounting for the human body in terms of its habituation by will or subjugation to particular forms and rituals. Because this semiotic focus failed to redress the prevailing dichotomy of mind and body, I continued to see a theoretic frame that acknowledged the interdependence of mind, body, and activity, as well as the transformative potential of this partnership to enhance learning. I took interest in the work of Elizabeth Grosz (1994), who has argued the need for a theory of the human body that heeds at least five criteria,

> First, it must avoid the impasse posed by dichotomous accounts of the person which divide the subject into the mutually exclusive categories of mind and body. . . . Second, corporeality must no longer be associated with one sex (or race). . . . Third, it must refuse singular models . . . which are based on one type of body as the norm by which all others are judged. . . . Fourth, while dualism must be avoided, so too, where possible . . . must biologistic or essentialist accounts of the body. The body must be regarded as a site of social, political, cultural, and geographical inscriptions, production or constitution. Fifth, whatever models are developed must demonstrate some sort of internal or constitutive articulation . . . between the biological and the psychological, between the inside and the outside of the body. (21–22)

The significance of Grosz's theoretical project is her willingness to seek congruities across two paradigms, biological and cultural, that have long represented the human body in agonistic ways. Grosz's call for theoretical reform holds central importance to researchers of literacy, for whom a traditional preoccupation with language has limited concern for how knowledge emerges from bodily activity. What remains necessary is a wider appreciation for how bodily activity anchors language and thought. Expanding the notion of situativity, this study makes clear that bodily activity is central not just to how we understand ourselves and live our bodies but to how, in the broadest sense, we think.

Minding the body constitutes a theoretical, instructional, and ethical project that begins with undoing the places and unlearning the practices that aggravate the mind–body split this study calls into question. Among secondary and postsecondary students, reports of violence, substance abuse, sexual promiscuity, eating disorders, depression, and suicide suggest that the human body is a site of pain and injury for many young people. How might this change if we were to understand the body as vital to learning and thought? Perhaps greater appreciation for the interrelation of mind, body, and activity would position us to foster the embodied schemata central to forms of being and knowing our students most need. Inevitably, what teachers and learners do is central not just to who they are in relation to each other but to how and what they know.

Epilogue

At the conclusion of the 1995–1996 season, the Hawkeye women lost to Vanderbilt in the semifinal round of the NCAA Mideast Regional. They had achieved a 27–4 overall record, won the Big Ten Conference title with a 15–1 mark, and remained undefeated for the year in Carver-Hawkeye Arena. In the spring of 1996 only Karen Clayton graduated. The returning squad included four of five starters and promised continued good fortune. But in May, Stacy announced her desire to transfer to Iowa State University. At her request, the Iowa women's athletic director granted a release that allowed her to communicate with Iowa State athletic personnel. Among stunned Iowa coaches and administrative staff, there existed feelings of hurt. Stacy had not acknowledged thoughts about transferring until the formal release, at which time she had explained to the press her wish to play for her sister, who was an assistant women's basketball coach at Iowa State. The loss of Stacy was sudden and would have dramatic consequences for the teammates she left behind. While Iowa players knew that Stacy had desired more playing time her freshman year, they, too, were surprised by her departure.

After considerable instructional investment in Stacy's development, the Iowa coaches now faced an extraordinary loss at the crucial point guard position. Without Karen and Stacy, Nadine would be called upon to adjust, this time shifting back to the activity and corresponding conceptual orientation she had relinquished the year before. Losing Nadine at the off guard position meant fewer shooting opportunities from a player who had become a scoring leader. Now, Nadine would need to focus on orchestrating offensive and defensive sets. The associational adjustments would prove difficult for all players. On Media Day in mid-October of 1996, Coach Lee introduced a senior class that included Simone, Susan, and Jenny, a trio with limited career playing time. The seniors tried to reassure the press, but they were less than convincing. Simone remarked, "I have a lot of confidence in my knee. I love this knee. No matter how much pain I go through, I'm still here. Don't feel sorry for this poor Jamaican. I may not be 100 percent, but I'll be strong enough to last." Responding to questions about her own lack of playing time, Susan noted, "We're not about numbers. Everybody has different roles and responsibilities." Jenny, too, seemed hesitant, "The big picture can be very overwhelming if you think about it." Picked by conference coaches to win the Big Ten title, the senior class seemed already daunted by the prospect of defending their place. As the press corps fixated upon the lack of depth at the point guard position, Lee was frank, "People are going to question the point guard spot. I don't."

In mid-November, the Hawkeyes lost their second game of the season at home. In addition to seniors who lacked playing time and who did not occupy starting roles, Nadine continued to acculturate as players recalibrated their associations to each other. In early December, the team faced a three-game, four-day tournament in Hawaii. Worried about an impending finals week, Coach Lee had invited me to join the team to conduct study sessions on the road (I discuss the ethical dilemmas this invitation posed in the Afterword). Accompanying the team, I experienced several days that I would later understand as an almost surreal forewarning.

High winds jostled our stretch Boeing 757 across the Pacific, but that constituted only the beginning of a tempestuous four days. Arriving in Kona on December 5, players and coaches were informed that their luggage and equipment had been accidentally rerouted through San Francisco and would not arrive until the next afternoon. In darkness, players, coaches, and support staff boarded a bus for the thirty-minute drive to a hotel located at the far end of the Kohala Coast. En route, the bus driver, a native resident of the Big Island, was a repository of lore. At one point on the desolate, unlit highway, he turned to Coach Lee and remarked, "I could tell you stories that make your skin crawl." At that, Nadine scooted into the seat directly behind the driver, a move that cued the story of Pueo, a native owl with the power to foreordain futures.

On December 6, the team practiced in their travel clothes. High winds combined with humidity left players and coaches edgy. In lopsided victories the next two days, the Hawkeyes defeated Boise State and Pacific, though dehydration left them nauseous during and after each game. Against Boise State, Amy scored 40 points to lead the Hawkeyes to a lopsided 89–34 victory, the third largest margin of victory in the history of Iowa women's basketball. Against Pacific, Susan scored a career-high 14 points and Jenny a career high number of assists.

While the new leaders were exciting, there was a disturbing lopsidedness to play. Unlike the previous year, points originated from fewer shooters. In the third and final game of the tournament, the Hawkeyes lost to Nebraska, a defeat that stunned the coaches. Though two earlier losses had pointed to chinks in players' associations with each other, I had no insights to offer Coach Lee when she solicited my interpretation of the Nebraska loss. On the return flight to Los Angeles, turbulence was again severe. Dispersed throughout the plane, players and coaches remained immobilized in their seats, unable by the lack of proximity to speak and by the wrenching jolts to sleep. In Los Angeles, Coach Myers learned that travel glitches would force the team to take the last leg of their trip from Chicago not by plane but by bus. By the time the team finally returned to Iowa City, players and coaches were frustrated and tense, a spirit that would last the duration of the season.

By December 28, the Hawkeyes were 4–4. Tangela had descended into profound anxiety. She would write in an essay for class, "I just can't do anything right. I play only to make mistakes, and I think that I am a total buster. I have lost all the confidence I ever had in one lousy season." Gripped by doubt, Tangela retreated into the interpretation of her play and positional knowledge, a shift that inhibited her capacity to think reflexively. In January, a rash of devastating injuries set in. By the end of the month, only Nadine had started every game of the season. Immobilized six games by knee injury, Tiffany struggled to recover. Knocked out for three games due to ankle injury, Simone would never regain momentum. Recovering from concussions and a hamstring injury, Angie Hamblin missed two games. And Malikah, reinjuring her knee, applied to the NCAA for yet another medical redshirt, a demoralizing request that would deflate her aspirations once and for all. While the Hawkeyes would win the last seven of eight conference games, they would never return to the conceptual solidarity of the 1995–1996 season. Only by winning the Big Ten Conference Tournament did the team earn an NCAA tournament birth. Losing to Connecticut in the second round, the Hawkeyes ended the 1996–1997 season with an overall record of 18–12 and a conference mark of 9–7.

Because I attended only a few practices during the 1996–1997 season, I was unable to observe the manner in which players negotiated their conceptual orientation. Clearly, physical and psychological pain disrupted the degree of trust players invested in their own bodies, as well as those of their teammates. Nadine's positional shift seemed a factor, too. Several months after graduating, Karen explained,

> Nadine has had a lot to learn this year. She has so much ability and talent that I don't think anybody is worried about how well she's going to do physically with it. She has to realize that she's the number one choice, and she has to play forty minutes. She's got to learn a lot

more situational things. Last year she was concerned with doing the play, getting open, getting the shot. Now it's shifting to assisting scoring production, being smart defensively and calling plays.

While Nadine was quick to assume responsibility for losses, this may well have undermined her authority among teammates who understood their own potential in terms of the command at the point. Certainly, losing the first five of eight home games of the season shook the faith of players who had lived a previous season in Carver-Hawkeye Arena without a loss. Home was no longer home.

In light of players' wavering faith, it may be that coaches assumed more authority for rituals and rehearsals than they had in the 1995–1996 season when the rights to ritual invention had allowed players to imagine their identity as a team. Whatever the various factors, the Iowa women did not recapture the spirit of the 1995–1996 season.

A year later, in the spring of 1998, the class who bore so much public expectation ended their intercollegiate careers with an overall senior season of 18-13 and a conference mark of 13–3. Momentum late in the season earned the Hawkeyes a birth in the NCAA tournament. Despite an impressive first round victory against the University of Massachusetts, the Hawkeyes would lose at home in the second round to the University of Kansas. Later that spring, following graduation, Tangela was a draft pick of the Sacramento Monarchs in the Women's National Basketball Association. Since then, during the winter months, she has played on professional teams in Sicily, Israel, and Turkey. Returning for her third season with the Monarchs in the summer of 2000, she was a candidate for the league's Most Improved Player award.

In her final season at Iowa, Simone averaged 4.5 rebounds and 8.6 points per game, enough to earn the attention of scouts for the New York Liberty, where she played in the WNBA's inaugural season. Simone— both knees braced—played subsequent winter seasons for a professional team in Jerusalem. In the 2000 season she started at center for the WNBA's Seattle Storm. Along with Tangela, Nadine joined the Sacramento Monarchs after her graduation from the University of Iowa. She has since played during the winter season for a professional team in Poland. Angie Hamblin signed a contract with the Detroit Shock and played six games before marrying and returning to Gary, Indiana, her hometown. Malikah did not return to basketball for the 1998–1999 Iowa season, though her scholarship allowed her to complete her degree. Following graduation, she lived and worked in Iowa City. During the 2000–2001 winter season, Malikah played professional basketball in Brazil. Graduates Shannon Perry, Karen Clayton, and Susan Koering hold assistant coaching jobs at the University of Southern California, Virginia Tech, and Ashland College (OH), respectively. After graduation and periodic stints on professional teams, Jenny Noll returned to her hometown of Muscatine, Iowa, where she has established a small business. Amy Herrig has entered graduate school in business at the University of Iowa, where Tiffany Gooden is enrolled in law school. Stacy Frese started at point guard at Iowa State University after the year of ineligibility following her transfer. During her senior season, she led the Cyclones to the NCAA Midwest Regional Semifinals. Following graduation, she and Amy spent the summer of 2000 playing for the WNBA's Utah Starzz.

Afterword

Reflexive Ethnography and the Undoing of a Scholarly Warrior

. . . a writer's subject positions are determined by the space of the body, her geographical location, her shifting intellectual positions, her distance or closeness to others, to texts, to events . . . ethos is created when writers locate themselves; it is "a way of claiming and taking responsibility for our positions in the world, for the ways we see, for the places from which we speak."

Nedra Reynolds,
"Ethos as Location"

Following Billy's departure from the university, I organized several semesters of independent study, at one point joining another graduate student and two professors to read and discuss key texts in performance studies (see Appendix B). During one session, Mary Trachsel, a faculty participant, shared a manuscript in progress, one in which she analyzed a recurring trope for academic publishers. Referring to the language that often characterizes press catalogs, she noted,

> The central metaphor for scholarly performance is the warrior role, the explorer-conquerer role. So, the more you can armor yourself, make yourself impenetrable, the less vulnerable you are to being unseated. I think it's there. In this article [points to the manuscript] I went through academic press catalogs and looked at the language they

117

used to advertise scholarly work. Look at this [reads from the draft], You "explore a world." It's a "powerful guide," "breaks new ground," "explores unknown territory," "reopens a path," "opens the way." It's a voyage of "great discovery." It takes us "over vast terrain." It's "an adventure." It "charts previous unexplored fields," "uncovers new strata," "sets out to make discoveries." This conquest. He's a "challenging writer who attacks basic structures," "confronts problems," "executes critical maneuvers," "takes a daring stand," "spearheads the dismantling of a subject," "rescues a subject," "breaks down barriers." . . . It's like you explore and conquer. You "stand unrivaled." It's a "tour de force." (Cheville et al. 1994, 69–70)

One must wonder about the source of this "rhetoric of conquest," particularly in light of the scholarly discourses that so often devalue the conceptual significance of the human body. Perhaps the trope is only a device that resonates with writers, publishers, and readers. Or perhaps the language implies something about the concrete experiences that situate the working lives and conceptual orientations of scholars. At the very least, for me, the trope suggested a need to consider how scholarly activity might be positioning me to understand intellectual discovery as a solitary unreflexive quest.

I understood, then, that my analysis of embodied cognition would need to include scrutiny of my own bodily activity as fieldworker and writer. While the tradition of reflexive anthropology had acquainted me with rhetorical problems that characterize the shift from fieldwork to writing, what was missing was some sense for how bodily shifts might influence a writer's actual conceptual orientation. In this chapter, I share the reflexive strategies I relied on to recognize and document shifts in my own bodily activity. Though these strategies did not resolve dilemmas, they assisted me to monitor the conceptual significance of my bodily place. In this Afterword, I recount my attempts to

- understand ethnography as performance,
- resist "communicative hegemony,"
- document my shifting embodiments, and
- scrutinize disciplinary conceptions of the body.

Understanding Ethnography as Performance

Prior to fieldwork, I understood ethnography not as an aesthetic or poetic endeavor but as a discursive and material process. My series of independent courses had introduced me to performance studies, and I relied upon the concept of performance to foreground the transparent contingencies that often prevent ethnographers from accounting for their own bodily activity and history. Anthropologist Richard Bauman (1977) suggests that "performance is an especially potent and heightened means of taking the role of the other and of looking back at oneself" (48). Performance-sensitive ethnography represents the capacity of informants to alert researchers to the influence, perhaps even intrusion, of their own embodied histories.

Performance, as I refer to it in this chapter, evolves from an interdisciplinary theoretic paradigm. Inspired initially by speech act theory and the ethnography of speaking, concern for communication as a performative phenomenon involved two foci: speech as situated communicative praxes and speech as stylized verbal art. During the 1960s, Erving Goffman (1959) encouraged a conceptual shift from strict typological analyses of recurring structural patterns composing speech encounters to a broader interest in how the relationship of speaker and audience configures "presentations of self."[1] Goffman's use of a proscenium stage metaphor to document "frontstage"/"backstage" behaviors exemplified an interest in "the way in which the individual . . . presents himself and his activity to others, the ways and the kinds of things he may and may not do while sustaining his performance before them" (1959, xi). Goffman's interest in performance as an emergent phenomenon brought him into conflict with conversational analysts who preferred to focus on the systematicity of verbal encounters (e.g., turn-taking patterns, frame analysis, features of utterance). Inevitably, his interest in ritual, along with Ray Birdwhistell's and Edward Hall's focus upon nonverbal behavior, prompted researchers to consider communication according to two dimensions of performative praxes: the verbal and nonverbal.

In the 1980s select anthropologists collaborated in texts and academic conferences to prompt crossdisciplinary interest in "performance studies," which has come to represent an avenue of cultural critique attentive to the following dimensions of social interaction: the dialogic relation of performers, the emergent nature of any performance event, performers as spatio-temporally situated, and performance—oral or written—as embodied. Increasingly, these dimensions encourage performance-sensitive ethnographers to document the material conditions of their bodies, noting, first, how they are located by race, gender, and other somatic features and, second, how these realities of body influence fieldwork and inscription. Anthropologist Johannes Fabian (1990) suggests that performance is "a more adequate description both of the ways people realize their culture and of the method by which an ethnographer produces knowledge about that culture" (18). What makes the transition from fieldwork to writing so problematic, as Vincent Crapanzano (1990) explains, is that the process of embodiment for scholars "may be so authoritative for the participants that they fall under the illusion that they have a fixed, a timeless, 'an objective' vantage point"

(288). In other words, our acculturation into orthodox research practices leads us to believe that disembodiment is not only possible but empirical. For this reason, understanding ethnography as a performative process encourages researchers, at the stages of fieldwork and writing, to consider how their embodied practices and histories as scholars and as human beings may lead them to ascribe normative value to what they observe.

Prior to writing, I had read Madeleine Blais's *In These Girls, Hope Is a Muscle*, a nonfiction bestseller about a high school girls' basketball team in Amherst, Massachusetts. Early in the book, Blais is forthright about her lack of sport experience and technical expertise. In her recollection of the final loss that preceded the season she observed, Blais writes of Coach Ron Moyer and the team,

> He knew he would be revisiting tonight's game compulsively to figure out why his kids, over and over, had failed to finish the play. They were dutiful, they worked hard. Several of them, not just Jamila, had the potential to be great. They would not easily forgive themselves for tonight's failure; that was his job.
>
> "Look, you kids couldn't screw up bad enough for me not to love you. I have two great daughters, and if I could have fifteen more, I know I could get them right here on this bus in the Amherst uniforms."
>
> Up until now, there had been a few sniffles but no raging displays. The mention of 'daughters,' however, inflamed them. Daughters: the word reverberated, hung in the trapped air like a ball wavering on the rim of a basket.
>
> First from one, then another, a wail arose, so that soon the entire bus, already overstuffed with gym bags and the bureaucracy of outerwear needed to endure winter, was further overtaken by full-scale sobs, a luxurious unstoppable lamentation. It was a stampede of tears. (1995, 18–19)

In this passage, Blais relies upon a rhetorical trope common to fiction, what DuPlessis (1985) identifies as "the romance plot." According to DuPlessis, such a trope "values sexual asymmetry, including the division of labor by gender" and "is based on extremes of sexual difference" (5). My point is not to question what Blais saw, but to underscore that what she apparently saw and chose to represent in text underscores the need for reflexive rhetorical strategies. My concern, regardless of audience, is that Blais textualizes her informants without interrogating the gendered performances they enact. Relying upon a Cartesian rhetoric that grafts the mind–body dichotomy onto gender, Blais seems to overlook the relation of her own bodily history as a female to the scene at hand. The result is an account that naturalizes the enactments of male reason and female passion. Instead of "writing against culture" (Abu-Lughod 1991, 10) in ways that reveal the cultural underpinnings of the moment, Blais remains well within the culture that has produced her and those she observes. The episode was one that reminded me of the need to find strategies that would disclose the influence of my embodied history as a white, middle-class woman. To this end, I chose to share my representations with informants.

Another text that became central to my unlearning of the scholarly warrior performance was Anne Haas Dyson's "The Case of the Singing Scientist: A Performance Perspective on the 'Stages' of School Literacy." Dyson's primary achievement in this article is awakening literacy researchers to early work in performance theory. Dyson's article, which reports on a year-long investigation of an urban K-1 classroom, focuses upon Jameel, a "nonmainstream" student whose behaviors as a writer and reader seem to trouble his adjustment to a workshop approach. Theoretically, Dyson (1992) draws upon the early work of Richard Bauman and Dell Hymes, sociolinguists who distinguished performance from communication. For both, "performance" was an aesthetic occasion, a condition quite apart from our everyday use of language. Dyson's piece is important because the distinction it places between performance and communication prompts disembodied inscription. Dyson explains her intent this way,

> As I will illustrate in this article, Jameel used school story writing events to perform, often exploiting the music—the rhythm and rhyme—of language while other class members, like Mollie, aimed more straightforwardly to communicate. (1992, 4)

Carving a distinction between performance and communication, Dyson assumes the formalized view of sociolinguists published a decade before her. In the end, this forces her to make subjective judgments about what does and does not constitute performance for Jameel. She writes, "His presentations were at times performative, and, at other times, straightforwardly communicative" (1992, 22). The problem for Dyson, and ultimately for her representation of Jameel, is that her embodied practices and history as a language user led her to codify verbal and nonverbal behavior in ways that did not recognize Jameel's verbal and nonverbal activity as communicative. Moreover, her embodiment as a researcher encouraged her to believe that she was positioned beyond the social theater that encompassed Jameel. From this "objective" position, Dyson believed she could distinguish those students who "communicated" from those who did not.

In the end, the distinction that Dyson carves between performer and communicator reflects nothing more than what reflexive performance theorists would now describe as conventional and unconventional performances. Because Mollie's embodied presentation dovetails with Dyson's own embodiment, its performative features are transparent. Hence, she is a communicator. But because Jameel's manner of performance is different, because his verbal and bodily activity approximates many of the features Dyson recognizes as aesthetic or verbal art, he is classified as a performer. Current performance theorists would suggest that both Mollie and Jameel perform but that they do so either in accordance or discordance with Dyson's embodied history.

Conceptual breakthroughs since the publication of Dyson's article discount any attempt on the part of researchers to posit their bodies outside performances of which they are a part. As Elyse Pineau (1994) states,

> Performance combines full body engagement with critical reflexivity; information must be engaged somatically as well as intellectually. It is the dialectical process of doing and reflecting, experiencing and interpreting that distinguishes performance methodology from simply "acting out." (17)

In her comprehensive investigation of the lives of impoverished women and children of a northeastern Brazilian shantytown, Nancy Scheper-Hughes (1993) came to understand how Anglo-American feminist explanations of the maternal body failed to represent the "somatic culture" she witnessed, and to a lesser degree experienced, during fieldwork.[2] Much of Scheper-Hughes's *Death without Weeping: The Violence of Everyday Life in Brazil* captures her experience of re-embodiment during various periods of fieldwork among the women and children of the Alto de Cruzeiro. The book exists as a model to those who seek methodologies and rhetorics that facilitate an embodied ethnographic stance.

Laurel Richardson (1994) suggests that anthropologists are "homogenized through professional socialization" to assume the "omniscient voice of science" (517). Those who publish, those who receive grants, and those who achieve tenure often must give in to the discourse conventions of the academy or risk exclusion. My interest is in what the collusion between ethnographer and her academic community means to those she represents in text. In the *Anthropology Newsletter* of January 1994, three anthropologists employed by the Hopi Tribe raise ethical concerns that warrant attention. Repeated distortion of Hopi culture by outside scholars has led the tribe to participate more actively in its own representation. According to the authors, "While recognizing the value of some of this research, many Hopi feel that much of that research was conducted under false pretenses for the personal gain of non-Indian scholars who benefit financially and professionally from the publications they write" (Dongoske et al. 1994, 56). The case of the Hopi underscores the danger of all ethnographic research. Those most important to ethnographers during fieldwork can be misrepresented in text. Where fieldwork, at best, locates performances of ethnographer and informant on the same spatio-temporal plane, textual representation severs that context and creates another. In response to the ethical dilemmas inherent in that bodily and conceptual shift, the Hopi tribe enacted a review process summarized this way,

> On every project sponsored by the Hopi Tribe, the professional ethics of anthropology have to be assessed and reconciled with the ethics and values of the Hopi Way—the collection and use of field data obtained in ethnographic interviews must be done so as not to violate either the individual informant's trust, privileged clan or religious knowledge, or the culture and the beliefs of the Hopi people. (Dongoske et al. 1994, 57)

Some may argue the tribe's review system, an attempt to protect the Hopi people against misrepresentation, is a problematic form of censorship. To slip into that debate is to overlook a fundamental issue, the extent to which informants are allowed to name and negotiate their "other," in this case, the ethnographer.

Resisting "Communicative Hegemony"

Prior to this study, my tutorial relationship with Billy led me to think deeply about conceptual disjunctures arising from one's bodily activity and history. As I reported in the introduction, with the injury his junior year, Billy began to feel alienated from school, sport, and peers. At that time I had begun to wonder if Billy might regain a sense of power and autonomy by talking about his literacy struggle as an African American student athlete enrolled in a predominantly white Division I university. As I told him, I had recently completed Christopher Lee and Rosemary Jackson's *Faking It: A Look into the Mind of a Creative Learner*. Though Lee, a white student athlete on the University of Georgia's swim team, spoke to the pressures of collegiate sport, his struggle had little in common with Billy's. As an African American student athlete in a major revenue sport, Billy's experiences had been different. I encouraged Billy to think about the possibility of working together on a project that might deepen existing portraits of intercollegiate athletics.

Billy and I decided to meet once a week to talk about these dilemmas and to tape our conversations in the event we might eventually capture them in print. Though I had concerns with the idea of co-authorship, I preferred to think that issues of colonization were more rhetorical than experiential. In other words, until Billy and I confronted the vexing question of how our voices might be textualized, I believed our conversations would evolve as they always had. But I was wrong. Now, in possession of a tape recorder, I embodied a role that shifted my relation to Billy. My voice suddenly directed conversations, suggesting what Briggs (1984) describes as the fieldworker's "communicative hegemony."

Billy: I mean, I've been asking you sometimes, "Am I talking right? Am I telling you what you really want to know?" Sometimes I just feel that I'm saying things that's not making any sense or might not even be clear to you. I feel like I'm just talking.

Julie: Um hmm

Billy: Just blabbering. It's not really meaning anything. That's sometimes how a white teacher makes me feel.

Julie: You must sort of wonder about this project. You know, the fact that I'm white makes it sort of weird . . .

Billy: It's not weird. No, it's not that it's weird. It's just that if you are genuine. Sometimes I had that question come up. Are you really genuine with your intentions? And I think that you are, you know? I really believe that you are. So, at least until you prove me wrong. [Laughs]

Billy's questions were particularly acute. How "genuine" was my performance and how might I perform differently once he disclosed what he believed? Such skepticism after over two years of work together signaled a significant change. With its sudden authorizing intent, my voice somehow necessitated the need in Billy to "talk right," to embody knowledge a certain way—my way. Acknowledging my connection to white teachers who had historically elicited self-doubt, Billy diagnosed a fundamental shift in our working relationship. No longer a tutor who played the middle ground between sport and school, I had entered into a new set of bodily and verbal activity, with intents and purposes that were not only less clear but potentially dangerous. Had I been more attentive to the pressure Billy felt to "talk right," his attempt to act upon me, I might have rethought my efforts to involve Billy in a project that I considered therapeutic. As my relationship with Billy changed (from tutor, to co-writer, to writer), I consolidated authority in ways that may well have aggravated his understanding of himself.

Documenting Shifting Embodiments

From my experiences with Billy, I understood the need to think reflexively about my embodiments as fieldworker and writer. I knew, as well, that such a project would be labor intensive, requiring much time to counter the scholarly tradition that leads many to believe that what they observe and textualize is somehow disembodied. To this end, I decided upon a two-year period of data collection. During the first year, I concentrated on refining a fieldnote procedure. This involved intensive notetaking during daily practices, followed by several hours of writing once I had returned home after team breakfast. Every morning at my word processor, I synthesized handwritten fieldnotes with a second layer of reflexive analysis. Richard Schechner's (1982) workshop-rehearsal process guided my fieldnoting.

> Workshop-rehearsal passes through three distinct steps that coincide with the ritual process: 1) separation, or stripping away, reducing or eliminating or setting aside "me"; 2) initiation, or revelation, or finding out what's new in "me" or in/from another, or what's essential and necessary; and 3) reintegration, or building up longer and longer meaningful strips of behavior; making something for the public— preparing to reenter the social world but as a new and/or different self. The time spent in these three steps and the place where this work is done are liminal. (66)

Writing my way through these three steps was a way to identify my own transition from an academic habitus that privileged a disjuncture between body and mind to a field habitus that insisted upon their integration. Each morning of the first year I contemplated not simply what I had sensed and described on the court but, additionally, how I had been shaped by those who were heightening my awareness of an ever-changing "me." As a teacher, writer, former athlete, and coach, middle-aged, middle-class white woman, I had experienced a range of bodily practices from which conceptual orientations had emerged. Monitoring my embodied history would be necessary if I was not to ascribe normative value to the embodiments that dovetailed with my own.

As a result of this introspective engagement, my reentry into the field, whether it occurred later in the day or the next morning at practice, involved the presentation of a "different self." My departure from the scholarly body was slow and certainly complicated by bodily activity that distinguished me from those I was studying. As Emerson et al. (1995), note,

> . . . the ethnographer remains a stranger as long as, and to the extent that, she retains commitment to the exogenous project of studying the lives or understanding the lives of others—as opposed to the indigenous project of simply living a life in one way or another. (35)

During practices, I occupied a chair at the only courtside table available each morning for writing, the "officials" desk just off court and perpendicular to the center line. Despite its advantages as a place to observe participants' learning, I was not so peripheral that players completely overlooked my presence. During the first season of practices when I was actively notetaking, a bodily affirmation of my purposes and desires, a few players seemed content to remain distant. This was no doubt complicated by my interactions with coaches, who used the officials' desk as a repository for car keys, coffee mugs, sweatsuit jackets, and practice outlines. During water breaks, the coaches would sometimes return to the officials' desk, where my connections to institutional power were certainly clear to players. For any athlete, coaches hold significant power. In short, they determine who plays and who doesn't. That some student athletes preferred a polite but perceptible distance was certainly understandable. In effect, my scholarly performances (observation, notetaking, and interviewing) preempted what Johannes Fabian terms "coevalness," "a common, active 'occupation,' or sharing of time" (1993, 31).[3]

During the second season of my study, my performance as a note-taking observer gave way entirely to that of voluntary academic tutor. Understanding significantly more about the student athletes' embodiments on the court, I was no longer dependent upon alienating field-work practices. In effect, I became what Yamamoto (1979) terms a "service member," existing "as a helping hand who contributes to the survival and maintenance of the culture space" (39). By the beginning of the second competitive season, I was increasingly involved in the academic lives of participants. I held academic appointments in my office, in players' apartments and dorm rooms, and in my own apartment. In mid-November Coach Lee requested that I accompany the team on an extended road trip scheduled a week before semester examinations. She worried that the trip would interrupt students' academic progress and hoped that I might join the team, conducting study sessions and tutoring on the road. The team would be departing for the Kona Classic in Hawaii on a Thursday and play three games in three days before leaving the Big Island following a Sunday game. The players would return to face two hectic weeks of final projects and examinations.

Assisting the team as Coach Lee requested, and as several of the players wished, would raise certain ethical dilemmas for me. I worried that the trip would jeopardize my scholarly performance. Might not some readers have cause to wonder about my capacity to think and write critically when, at the same time, I was traveling at the expense of the women's athletic department? After assessing the academic needs of players and discussing the trip with colleagues, I chose to recognize my consequential presence and accompany the team. I felt it unethical to swerve from my service role at a time when student athletes required it most. Addressing the ethics of performance, Carol Benton (1993) writes,

> For performance practitioners, performing is not a luxury. It, too, is a way of being in the world, a way of critique, a way of responding, a way of engaging with self and other, and a way of engaging with its own, albeit unnamed, act of ethical and moral obligations. (100)

Ultimately, my shifting embodiment during the second year of field-work led me to scrutinize orthodox research procedures that deny informants the right to be actors and excuse ethnographers from service to informants.

Late the second year, as I began the writing process, I experienced yet another shift in embodiment. By this time, I had entered into relationships of mutual reliance. Players granted audiotaped interviews so that I might pose questions. Later, they read chapters, providing important suggestions for revision as well as approving those passages in which they appeared. Nadine encouraged me to "make us interesting," and I thought deeply about how a text might do that and still fulfill scholarly conventions. I understood that "pulling out" of fieldwork in some clean fashion was never possible nor my desire. But the traditional scholarly performance requires the ethnographer to conclude fieldwork and pull away from the temporal plane she has shared with informants. Decisions about textual representation suddenly demand foremost attention to the reader. And herein lies the problem. Where fieldwork obliges the ethnographer to access the bodily and conceptual orientation of informants, textual representation severs that dialog and creates another.

Scrutinizing Disciplinary Constructions of the Body

> . . . as a Black woman, I have always been acutely aware of the presence of my body in those settings that, in fact, invite us to invest so deeply in the mind/body split so that, in a sense, you're almost always at odds with the existing structure, whether you are a Black woman student or professor. But if you want to remain, you've got . . . to remember yourself—because to remember yourself is to see yourself always as a body in a system that has not become accustomed to your presence or to your physicality.
>
> bell hooks, *Teaching to Transgress*

As I scrutinized my own embodied location in the academy and continued to envision a theory of embodiment honoring both body and mind, I felt repeatedly stymied by a dearth of scholarship in embodied cognition. Another phase of my unlearning would involve a deepening sense for how academic disciplines have historically sustained the mind–body split this study calls into question. "Remembering" the history of the body in academic discourse became a way for me to interrogate my own theoretical location. In remembering the body, which is always a means of insisting upon its existence, I came to understand how sanctioned discourses of the body had cohered. To a large degree, this process of legitimization took place during the first three decades

of this century when a swelling alliance of universities, private philanthropic organizations, and governmental and industrial agents effectively recast the mind–body split as an intelligence–race polemic that
distinguished the "rational" white mind from the "primordial" body. In
effect, this alliance provided a means and a rationale for institutionaliz-
ing particular rhetorics and representations of the human body. From
the body as biological organism, I encountered other theoretical constructions of the human body that led me to think about how particular discursive traditions might frustrate my attempts to theorize and
document cognition as situated in bodily activity.

The Body as a Biological Construct

During the late nineteenth and early twentieth centuries, as most academic disciplines in the natural and social sciences began to solidify
within distinct university departments, the human body was considered a biological phenomenon. Darwinian conclusions about the "origin" and "descent" of "man" as an evolutionary creature had replaced
earlier polygenic theories that asserted "the doctrine of human races as
separate species" (Gould 1981, 43). Though Charles Darwin's theory of
evolution would lessen the Cartesian gap by its argument that the mind
as well as the body were biological constituents of the human organism,
Darwin's lack of specificity about the role of race allowed his successors
to use the concept of evolution as a means of asserting an ideal, hereditary form.[4]

   In 1883 Francis Galton, a cousin of Darwin, relied upon the principles of evolution and biological inheritance to issue his claim that
natural scientists should invest in the opportunity to control heredity.
Galton (1884) inspired the term *eugenics*, a translation of the Greek *well-
born*, thereby igniting interest in the possibility of biological interven-
tion (Degler 1991). One of Galton's earliest projects was his "beauty
map," a crude numerical survey of feminine beauty in the British Isles.
In the report, Galton characterized his method,

> Whenever I have occasion to classify the persons I meet into three
> classes, "good, medium, bad," I use a needle mounted as a pricker,
> wherewith to prick holes, unseen, in a piece of paper, torn crudely
> into a cross with a long leg. I use its upper end for "good," the cross
> arm for "medium," the lower end for "bad." The prick holes keep dis-
> tinct, and are easily read off at leisure. The object, place, and date are
> written on the paper. I used this plan for my beauty data, classifying
> the girls I passed in streets or elsewhere as attractive, indifferent, or re-
> pellent." (qtd. in Gould 1981, 75)

Galton's procedures, undoubtedly suspect, do suggest one of the problems with numerical research, primitive as it was then and sophisticated as it seems now, namely the designation of reference standards.

The eugenics movement in Europe and the United States argued that features of the body constituted the primary source for speculation about the mind. One of the founding proponents of eugenic thought in this country was Charles B. Davenport who, at the turn of the century, as an instructor in zoology at Harvard, became acquainted with the work of Karl Pearson, Galton's primary successor in England. By 1904, Davenport had orchestrated an endowment from the Carnegie Institution of Washington to establish a research station for the investigation of eugenic principles (Kevles 1984, 99). Where Galton and Pearson had relied upon phenotypic analyses (the study of observable traits), Davenport conducted genotypic exploration (the study of genetic traits) according to recently rediscovered tenets of Mendelian genetics. In effect, as Kevles describes, Davenport would depart from the "positive eugenics" agenda of Galton and Pearson, advocating a "negative eugenics." The British eugenics movement, to some extent a platform for social radicals, possessed a distinct utopian quality, the desire to experiment with heredity as a means to create a new and, in their minds, more "equitable" world.

Davenport's supervision of the eugenics research station at Cold Spring Harbor (Long Island) initiated numerous projects. One of the earliest was an investigation of "wayward" girls that found that "the cause of prostitution was not economic or experiential circumstance but an 'innate eroticism,' determined by a dominant Mendelian element" (Kevles 1984, 109). But Davenport's most influential work was undoubtedly the creation of the Eugenic Record Office, funded philanthropically by Mrs. E.H. Harriman, who upon her husband's death had become the executor of his railroad profits. With additional monies from John D. Rockefeller, Jr., the Eugenics Record Office began a professional externship program that would train fieldworkers to conduct eugenic research. The program became a primary clearinghouse for eugenic data. As Kevles describes,

> After the summer training course, the trainees, at a salary of seventy-five dollars a month, began a year's work in the field. . . . Once trained, they were armed with a "Trait Book" for guidance and sent to study albinos in Massachusetts; the insane at the New Jersey State Hospital in Matawan; the feebleminded at the Skillman School, in Skillman, New Jersey; the Amish in Pennsylvania; the pedigrees of disease in the Academy of Medicine records in New York City; and juvenile delinquents at the Juvenile Psychopathic Institute of Chicago. (1984, 114)

From these sites, most trainees returned either to university doctoral programs, to university appointments in the natural and social sciences, or to supervisory posts in various penal institutions. Across public and private spheres, eugenic thought became the means by which academic, commercial, and political spheres responded to the migration of

African American Southerners, to the continuing arrival of immigrant populations, and to pervasive social problems that accompanied dramatic urban growth.

By 1910 speculation about the inheritance of racial features and their link to intelligence served to marginalize immigrants newly arrived from central and southern Europe. In *The Passing of the Great Race*, Madison Grant (1916) warned that the influx of central and southern Europeans threatened to dilute the "great race" of Americans of northern European extraction. Following World War I, Grant would advise the Rockefeller Foundation in funding of anthropological projects. By World War I, assessment of the body according to observable racial and ethnic features and other more "scientific" procedures, like use of the cephalic index, had become the primary means of assessing intellect. Yet it was not until the application of intelligence tests to military personnel during World War I that psychologists would "prove" lower test scores of immigrants and African Americans. Writing of Lewis Terman, the Stanford professor who first revised Alfred Binet's intelligence scale, Paul Chapman (1988) notes,

> He [Terman] strongly believed that exams such as his Stanford-Binet and the National Intelligence Tests were valid and reliable measures of ability and that intelligence remained relatively constant. Convinced of the essential correctness of Galton's theories on hereditary genius and based on his own research with the gifted, he concluded that intelligence was greatly controlled by genes and was but little influenced by other factors . . . he decided early in his work that test score differences among ethnic, national, and occupational groups could be explained primarily in terms of inherited intelligence. (129)

Decades later extensive examination of these early intelligence assessments, and those that followed, would prove their inherent cultural bias. The traditional assumption of psychometrics reflected in the work of Terman and Yerkes is that innate intelligence is a quantity that can be measured [in isolate from] embodied histories of examiners and examinees.

By the mid-1920s, the academic disciplines, particularly psychology and the human sciences, had already configured according to the early conclusion that intelligence and race were biologically linked and bodily apparent. Such a view was important to major philanthropists of the period. According to Stocking (1992),

> Insofar as it expressed a generalized concern with the composition, quality, and control of the population of a complex industrial society, this postwar distillation of the progressive impulse may easily be interpreted as an ideological expression of the class interests of leading groups within a maturing corporate capitalist system. (184)

Ultimately, eugenic thought was the means by which higher education would serve a class elite in creating social, political, and economic policies that facilitated corporate capitalism, thereby expediting the transition from an agrarian to an industrial economy.

Increasingly after World War I, faculty members entered into alliances with private and corporate funding sources that recognized the social, political, and financial import of appropriating the issue of intelligence and other eugenic interests. It is important to note that the involvement of higher education in eugenic research was regionally defined. Southern universities did not play a significant role in the alliance of institutions that oversaw research and policy decisions. According to Larson (1995),

> By any measure, higher education lagged in the Deep South. At the turn of the century, the entire region had about half as many professors as did the state of Indiana, and less than one-twelfth as many graduate students enrolled in all of its schools as were enrolled at the University of Chicago. The annual income of all the region's colleges and universities then totaled approximately $850,000, which was significantly less than that of Harvard University alone. (40)

As Larson suggests, scientific research in southern states was substantially inhibited by a lack of money and technological resources. Despite an agrarian economy, which assisted northern universities in their investigation of Mendelian genetics, southern states simply lacked the means to conduct competitive research. That is not to say, however, that the eugenic movement failed at the grassroots level. The philanthropist Clarence Gamble established "dozens of subsidized sterilization clinics serving the poor of both races in the South . . . " and created a "Negro Project" that specifically targeted African Americans for "education" on birth control (Larson 1995, 156). What the eugenic movement in higher education indicates is regional investment in biological theories of the body. Ivy League institutions, as well as northern public universities from the Atlantic to the Pacific, represented primary contributors to eugenic-based research that promoted a direct correspondence between phenotypic and genotypic traits.

By the late 1920s, eugenic principles were actively legislated in state and federal mandates that involved sterilization of incarcerated populations, educational reforms, and immigration restrictions. In response to intelligence test results, terms like "ability grouping," "homogeneous grouping," and "tracking" became familiar words in the educational lexicon of the 1920s. As Arthur Applebee (1974) suggests, "The teacher, the philosopher, the administrator—each imitated the scientist; and though in fact their science was sharply limited by their training and the primitive state of the disciplines to which they turned for guidance, their conclusions shaped—and continue to shape—much educational practice" (80). By the end of the 1920s, the culmination of a "decade of progress," eugenic principles had driven deep institutional reforms.

The international popularity of eugenic research would culminate in the 1935 International Congress for Population Science in Berlin. Several influences contributed to the close rapport among German and American eugenicists, which developed following World War I. First, Davenport's Cold Spring Harbor Laboratory, specifically the collection methods of its Eugenic Record Office, offered vital methodological assistance to German officials interested in establishing wide-scale data collection in their own country. Harry Laughlin, an assistant to Davenport, would become the primary liaison, providing German researchers with methodological assistance as well as model legislation for the enactment of sterilization laws. Second, direct financial support of German eugenicists by the Rockefeller Foundation in New York continued even after the National Socialists assumed power in 1933 (Kuhl 1994, 21).

Kuhl's investigation of the ideological connections between the American eugenics movement and the German racial hygiene policies of National Socialism relies upon German archival sources that were of obviously little interest to those American eugenicists disinvolving themselves from association with German racial hygienicists after the full extent of Nazi methods became clear. Kuhl draws upon archival sources in Germany that point to notable American interest in the German program. As the 1930s wore on, American eugenicists faced the growing criticism of dissenting academics. Though many of these academics were vocal, they lacked institutional connections to money and resources, a fact that diminished their capacity to attack what had become a pervasive movement. Nevertheless, a host of cultural anthropologists, biologists, and geneticists continued their criticism until the Nazi escalation of anti-Semitic legislation finally forced American eugenicists to redefine their intellectual position.

The Body as a Cultural Construct

For scholars interested in the human body as a bearer of cultural influence, the work of anthropologist Franz Boas remains fundamentally important. Boas's research, his teaching, and his vocal criticism of the eugenic movement were part of his larger mission to challenge the construction of the human body as strictly biologic. Boas's theoretical allegiance hearkened back to Alfred Wallace, a contemporary of Darwin's who concurred that natural selection was a feature of human development but that evolutionary distinctions between human cultures was not. In short, Wallace explained differences among races as cultural rather than evolutionary. It was not until 1911 that Boas would appropriate a cultural explanation of difference. The same year that Charles B. Davenport published *Heredity in Relation to Eugenics*, Boas produced *Changes in the Bodily Form of Descendants of Immigrants*, which suggested that scientists had significantly underestimated the influence of culture upon the development of the body. Hired by the federal government to direct a study of immigrant populations, Boas established baseline data with available techniques of the time.

Relying upon the cephalic index, a measurement of the "ratio of the length to the width of the human head" (Degler 1991, 63), Boas collected data on thousands of immigrant families in New York City. As Degler explains,

> The results were surprising even to him [Boas]. For they showed that the head shapes of children of immigrants changed after the mother had been in the United States for a period of time. In fact, the changes in this alleged stable measure occurred within ten years after the mother's arrival in the American environment. Since the genetic input was identical—the mothers and fathers were the same— the social environment must have been the source of the changes. (1991, 63)

Specific features that characterized ethnic populations underwent changes toward a common type. Boas argued that the "plasticity" of the human body rendered the mind susceptible to environmental influence. The fact that the cranial dimensions of those children measured had altered toward a common cephalic ratio suggested that environmental influences held conceptual significance.

Boas's conception of the body as a cultural construct stood in stark contrast to the eugenic construction. The Boasian form implied an integration of brain and body regardless of ethnic or racial type. As a first-generation Jewish immigrant, Boas's personal and professional convictions converged in a teaching and research career that would address the underpinnings of racist scientific and social policies. As a researcher, Boas entered into professional relationships that deepened his conviction that culture was a vital, mitigating influence on conceptual development. As an academic, Boas strove to promote intercultural understanding, lobbying hard for Carnegie funds that might establish a museum of African American culture. When Andrew Carnegie declined, Boas began to shape the department of anthropology at Columbia in ways that would foster investigations of race and culture (Stocking 1992). By the mid-1920s, he was supervising numerous students who came to Columbia expressly for that purpose. Among them, Zora Neale Hurston whose *Mules and Men* is a rich ethnographic study of her native Florida.

During the 1930s, Boas would become "the most prominent critic of Nazi race policy" (Kuhl 1994, 80). Within the sphere of higher education, Boas attempted to unite a cross-section of scientists against Nazi racial policies. But support for eugenic principles proved formidable. Ambivalence existed among scientists who seemed willing to watch the unfolding of eugenic policy in Germany. Following the 1937 International Population Congress in Paris, Boas challenged eugenic scholarship among social scientists. Most preferred only to refute the German promotion of Aryan superiority. To many, Boas was an irritant. According to Stocking, his public comparisons between Nazi anti-Semitism and American racism preceded his "censure and removal from office in the American Anthropological Association" (1992, 105). Until his death in 1942, "Boas's emphasis was on attacking racial propaganda, and, characteristically, he felt that 'the only way to attack the racial craze that is sweeping the world nowadays is to undermine its alleged scientific basis'" (Stocking 1992, 108).

Shortly before Boas's death, Melville Herskovits published *The Myth of the Negro Past*, an extension of his mentor's stance on culture and race. His substantive analysis of African American culture is emblematic of the attempt nearly all Boas's students made to document a cultural, rather than biological, conception of the body. That Herskovits was overlooked in the Carnegie search for a director to oversee a massive project on "the American Negro" suggests the reluctance private philanthropies continued to reserve for such an approach to race. In the end, Gunnar Myrdal would be designated project director. Published in the mid-forties, the resulting *An American Dilemma*, though critical of deterministic theories, represents an interesting counterpoint to Herskovits's *The Myth of the Negro Past*.

Ultimately the principles of cultural anthropology spread through the teaching and research of Boas's students. As Richard Fox (1991) suggests, various foci would arise from the central Boasian concern for culture. Whereas early Boasians focused on the historical integration of cultures "as collections of cultural traits" (103), later Boasians like Mead and Benedict focused on the psychical relation of individual to culture. Though the post-war climate involved greater receptivity to cultural explanations, many philanthropic financiers proceeded with caution, believing cultural approaches lacked scientific credibility. Post-war attention accorded to the work of Claude Levi-Strauss suggests the degree to which the scientific fascination with the "savage" other still found favor. In the end, what Boasian anthropology achieved would be due in large measure to the dogged, underfinanced pursuits of those who operated in the interstices of a corporate funding system that primarily subsidized anthropology as a natural science.

Qualitative research in education has yet to revive the Boasian interest in the body as the interface between culture and cognition. In my view, the foundations of this tradition support current scholarship in embodied cognition. Avoiding the divide between mind and body, which was a source of ideological grafting for eugenic researchers, Boas exhibited concern for the propensity of one's "biology" to adapt to cultural influence. More recently, neurologist Antonio Damasio has blurred the boundaries of biology and culture, arguing that cultural influences shape the interdependence of mind and body.

> (1) The human brain and the rest of the body constitute an indissociable organism, integrated by means of mutually interactive bio-chemical, and neural regulatory circuits . . . ; (2) The organism interacts with the environment as an ensemble: the interaction is neither of the body alone nor of the brain alone; (3) The physiological operations that we call mind are derived from the structural and functional ensemble rather from the brain alone: mental phenomena can be fully understood only in the context of an organism's interacting in an environment. That the environment is, in part, a product of the organism's activity itself, merely underscores the complexity of interactions that we must take into account. (1994, xvi)

Refusing to conceptualize the human body according to an erroneous separation from mind, Damasio sidesteps the nature vs. nurture debate, underscoring the plasticity of the human body as it is located within culture. To the extent that Damasio's work inspires interdisciplinary discussion of the human body as a holistic construct and to the extent it inspires collaborative research projects, it may lay the ground for interdisciplinary studies of embodied cognition.

The Body as a Sociolinguistic, Sociocognitive, and Sociocultural Construct

Post-war discoveries of the Nazi eugenic program brought dramatic restraint to how American scholars pursued and promoted their investigations of the human body. In 1964, with the passage of the Economic Opportunity Act, the American public witnessed federal investment in the debate on literacy. One result was renewed interest in issues of language and poverty, including the extent to which the two conditions were interrelated. Urban language studies were beginning to indicate that any theory of literacy that explained failure according to assertions of verbal or intellectual deficit was ideologically suspect, hearkening back to a eugenic tradition of racial and ethnic prejudice. Most provocative of these urban investigations was William Labov's *The Logic of Non-Standard English* (1969), which challenged the findings of previous studies conducted in South Central Harlem by representatives of the United States Office of Education. Federally-sponsored research, like nearly all educational studies conducted prior to and during the 1960s, created asymmetrical interview conditions that favored physical and social conventions of the researchers themselves.

In the government-sponsored studies Labov cited, middle-class linguists, additionally white and male, interviewed children from south-central Harlem one at a time in an unfamiliar room. Findings argued that the language of "culturally deprived children" discouraged their development, not just as users of language but as logical thinkers. In fact, linguists' disregard for their own performances, namely for the physical and interactional constraints they imposed upon the children, led to inaccurate conclusions about the children's linguistic and intellectual aptitude. Failing to consider the bodily dimensions of their inquiry, these researchers had created an interview situation that intimidated participants. Restructuring the interview situation in ways that accommodated the verbal and nonverbal practices of the subjects, Labov found that the children he interviewed were far from monosyllabic and illogical.

By the end of the 1960s, many universities and colleges were revising admission policies according to federal mandates designed to insure equal educational opportunities for minority students. Not coincidentally, these changes in the structure of higher education were accompanied by a resurgence of eugenic thought that revived the view that intelligence test scores were a product of cultural and intellectual deficit. Hudson (1972) has noted that hereditary claims about race and intelligence often accompany historical periods in which minority groups experience social and economic opportunity.[5]

According to Kevles (1984), the individual perhaps most responsible for "the new eugenics movement" was Arthur B. Jensen, a professor of educational psychology at the University of California-Berkeley. Appearing in the *Harvard Education Review* the same year as Labov's publication, Jensen's "How Much Can We Boost IQ and Scholastic Achievement?" (1969) spurred numerous rebuttal articles and books. Considering the heritability of intelligence, scholastic achievement, and the influence of physical and social factors, Jensen noted that "identifiable" or racial groups appearing at various levels of "[the] educational, occupational, and socioeconomic hierarchy" suggest by their collective number a potential link between race and intelligence. The halted sale of the issue and a confusing process of rebuttal prevented empirical dispute of Jensen's argument, though scholars would eventually highlight its fallacies.

In its guidelines for research, the National Institute of Education recommended in 1974 that the study of language should accord more significance to "the social context of cognition" given that "speech unites the cognitive and the social" (qtd. in Cazden 1988, 2). This recommendation represented an important attempt to expand the focus of linguistic research. Instead of analyses that explicated prosodic, lexical, and grammatical features of single speakers, the National Institute of

Education (NIE) underscored the need for *socio*linguistic studies. A year later, psychologist Robert L. Williams published *Ebonics: The True Language of Black Folks,* employing a term that had arisen in conversation with other African American scholars two years earlier (Smitherman 1999). Conflating *ebony* and *phonics, ebonics* boldly asserted the interrelation of body and language. While its inventors were primarily concerned with establishing the ancestral relation of African American vernacular English to African languages, the term *ebonics* also foregrounds what few words in scholarly discourse do, that language and bodiliness are inseparably linked. I wonder if the relative disregard for the term then and now may reflect, to some degree, the scholarly resistance directed toward any suggestion that physicality shares a connection to language and cognition.

Linguistic and sociolinguistic investigations have positioned researchers to identify and defend language diversity. In her prolific writing and activism, linguist Geneva Smitherman has argued the legitimacy of ebonics, in 1979 assuming an influential role in the notorious Ann Arbor case that challenged the instructional practices of teachers who subjected elementary-age ebonics speakers to inappropriate and destructive remediation. In her landmark ethnography *Ways with Words* (1984), sociolinguist Shirley Brice Heath explored how classroom practices recognized and reproduced the linguistic and cultural traditions of middle-class children. Documenting the complex intersection of language, culture, and schooling, Smitherman and Heath show how intolerance for language diversity extinguishes learners' access to knowledge. For decades now, this work has inspired interest in how, across contexts, social activity situates thought. In their cumulative effect, both linguistic and sociolinguistic traditions have brought researchers to a place where concern for the body can begin.

In recent decades, numerous educational researchers have turned to the tradition of phenomenology and to the French historian Michel Foucault to explore the mitigating effects of social context upon individual learners. One of Foucault's important contributions was distinguishing how the body politic of various historical periods surveyed and disciplined individual human bodies. Across these periods, Foucault showed how cultural forms of discipline "produced subjected and practiced bodies, 'docile' bodies" (1984, 182). Foucault argued the influence of the body politic was both anatomical and metaphysical, reducing individual bodies to an abject condition from which their labor potential could be exploited to sustain and reproduce particular political conditions.

Though Foucault's work does lend itself to discussions of embodiment, the focus is primarily upon the supremacy of the body politic and its role in subordinating the behavior and thought of distinct human bodies. Essentializing the significance of culture and its generational effects, Foucault has assisted sociocultural researchers to identify how students, teachers, and classrooms are configured by material and discursive conditions. But Foucault's construction of the body is problematic. Devaluing subjective agency, Foucault grants the body primary significance as an object of cultural surveillance and discipline. According to Terence Turner,

> . . . what Foucault's notion of the body as an essential inert of passive conceptual category excludes is the body in its socially fundamental aspect as material activity, including the entire range of concrete bodily processes and faculties that are direct and effected with varying degrees of success, within the schemas of acting, perceiving, cognizing, and feeling. . . . (1994, 43)

For those who theorize learning as a bodily and conceptual process, Foucault does not account for the efficacious experience of emotion and agency that can result from the interdependence of mind and body.

Minding the Body in Text

> Self-adoration is quite different from self-awareness and a critical scrutiny of the self. Indeed those who protect the self from scrutiny could as well be labeled self-satisfied and arrogant in presuming their presence and relations with others to be unproblematic.
>
> Judith Okely, "History as Usual?
Feminism and the 'New Historicism'" (1992)

I have limited my analysis to select discourses of the human body that have evolved within the natural and social sciences. My point is that the recasting of the mind–body split into an intelligence–race polemic has, by institutional sanction, infiltrated certain disciplinary rhetorics. As a result, discussions of embodied cognition demand a new yet common language, one that relinquishes the obtuse natural and cultural terminology that has long been used to alienate critics. A theory of embodied cognition that recognizes the conceptual significance of bodily activity will hinge upon disciplinary compromise, collaboration, and vigilance. As Bryan Turner argues,

> To reject Cartesianism, it is not necessary to deny the corporeal nature of human existence and consciousness. To accept the corporeality of human life, it is not necessary to deny the fact that the nature of the human body is also an effect of cultural, historical activity. The body is both natural and cultural. (1984, 49)

Finally, a theory of embodied cognition will constitute an interdisciplinary hermeneutical project, one that welcomes the guiding principle of

embodied consciousness and rejects the historical tradition of catego-
rizing human bodies in the drive to consolidate and protect racial, ethnic, and class privilege. I hope for an interdisciplinary framework that
establishes common ground across disciplinary traditions that have
theorized the body as *object* (e.g., Marxism, feminism, psychoanalysis,
post-structuralism), as *subject* (phenomenology, existentialism, performance theory, liberation theology), and as *organism* (biomedicine, genetics, and psychology). Such a theoretic frame would restore significance to the body without collapsing into the splintered discourses that
have traditionally disrupted any comprehensive sense for what it means
to be and know.

For nearly ten years now as a writer and a teacher of writing, I
worry that theories of learning that essentialize the role of language
undercut the conceptual significance of the body. The reflexive strategies I share in this chapter represent my attempt to remember my body.
Though I was not writing autobiography, I did keep in mind Sidonie
Smith's (1993) notes on autobiographical method, which assisted me to
review my inscriptions of others.

> Whose history of the body is being written? What specific body does
> the autobiographical subject claim in her text? How and where does
> the autobiographical speaker reveal or conceal, give or withhold (or
> both) her identity or body, and for what purposes? Does the body drop
> away as a location of autobiographical identity, or does the speaker
> insist on its founding identification? What are the implications for
> subjectivity of the body's positioning? How is the body the performa-
> tive boundary between inner and outer, the subject and the world?
> What regulatory actions of the body politic impinge on the deploy-
> ment of the autobiographical body? How are other bodies arranged in
> the text? (23)

For me, Smith's questions were a way of foregrounding my scholarly
location in a nexus of competing theoretical constructions of the human
body. These questions, in combination with existing ethnographies that
document fieldwork as embodied practice, encouraged me to recognize
my place in scholarly discourse and to understand the implications of
that location for fieldwork and writing.[6]

Reflexive thinking and writing upend the mythic dichotomy between objective self and subjective other, instead affirming the contingencies of performance. That human beings are "mobile and mul-
tiply situated" (Marcus 1994, 566) strips ethnographers of an objective
stance. We are connected bodily to the contexts that have shaped us
and the contexts we study. What that means conceptually is something
for which we must begin to account. More sophisticated representations will demand a reflexive appreciation for how place, person, and
time configure the ethnographer's embodiment in the field and for how

the bodily shift to writing invites conceptual shifts that may lead us to resist or override the influence of informants. It may be that the fear of being cited as "self-indulgent," "confessional," or, worse yet, "narcissistic" is what most troubles reflexive writers. Because performance-sensitive ethnographers lack models, they tend to lack faith. They lack faith that change can be enacted within an academic culture that mandates the exertion of force in textual presentations of self. Perhaps there is no recourse but the understanding that effecting change will demand the resolve to read deeply, to converse often, and to write well.

Notes

1. John Lofland (1984) describes Goffman as "the first truly active discoverer" in American sociology (8). Certainly, Goffman's interest in ritual rather than language per se led to his conflicts with conversational analysts (Sacks, Schegloff, Jefferson) who preferred to study the systemic structure of language in interactional encounters. For Goffman, performance was a way of understanding in what manner ritual and language constituted the self. He considered performance to be "all the activity of a given participant on a given occasion which serves to influence in any way any of the other participants" (1959, 15). In effect, Goffman understood performance as primarily an issue of how effectively participants presented themselves to others as a means of fulfilling their own respective intentions. In light of current studies of performance, such a view is problematic for its hierarchical relation of performer to audience. Goffman was far less interested in the capacity of the audience to perform and of performance to emerge dialogically. Other themes from Goffman's work include the metaphor of the game and gamester; an emphasis upon naturalistic methodologies, namely ethnography; and a lasting interest in the ritual constraints that shape the self. While Goffman's work may allow us to understand how language and ritual shape the presentation and potentiality of selves, it less effectively assists theorists to document power as a diffusive element.

2. Nancy Scheper-Hughes (1993) suggests that the contexts of female embodiment in Western culture do not situate scholars, particularly those who argue a "female psychology" from locations of racial and class privilege, to understand or accurately represent the "somatic cultures" of second and third-world women.

3. Johannes Fabian (1993) explores how the temporal shifts that occur with the transition from fieldwork to writing influence an ethnographer's conceptual orientation. Fabian's work is centrally important to understanding ethnography as both embodied process and product.

4. See early hereditary arguments in Bean (1906), Brinton (1890), Cope (1887), Galton (1884), and Lombroso (1911).

5. For sources that revitalized "the new eugenics movement," see Eysenck (1971) and Richard Herrnstein (1971, 1994).

6. For reflexive ethnographies, see Behar (1993), Jean Briggs (1970), Lavie (1990), Myerhoff (1978), and Wolf (1992).

Appendix A: The Field Project

Field Project Rationale

In a recent article appearing in *The Chronicle of Higher Education*, a sociology professor at the University of California-Santa Barbara expressed concern for what he termed a nationwide "culture of disengagement" among college students. Professor Robert Flacks cited declining participation in organized campus activities as one of several indicators that point to students' growing detachment from academic life. This course arises from my belief that disengagement is dangerous and that much of my job as a faculty member is to encourage your critical understanding of this institution and its relation to your history as a learner.

This course is designed to engage you in the process of exploring cultural life on this campus. During the opening weeks of this semester, you will no doubt feel moments of insecurity, even fear, as you encounter other students. Because you are not yet an insider to any one group, you are in an excellent position to analyze human behavior and organization. As an outsider, you can perceive aspects of cultural life more vividly now than you will in several months. This course takes advantage of your etic, or outsider, perspective by introducing you to anthropological tools for the analysis of culture. These tools are useful in any context.

In this course, you must be willing to consider your own experience, language, values, and history in relation to a campus subculture you elect to study. Analyzing the cultural life of others is not about passing judgment but about "interpreting" features of cultural life for what they imply about individual and group identity. In this class you will learn anthropological techniques for analyzing the following features:

a. *artifacts*—objects people produce, share, possess, and display,

b. *place*—spaces people create, possess, share, and inhabit,

c. *rituals*—recurring behaviors people enact and redefine,

d. *language*—verbal and nonverbal language people use to interact, and

e. *stories*—narratives people rely upon to preserve their individual and collective identities.

The semester-long field project you will design and conduct in this class will allow you to investigate a campus subculture of personal or professional interest. At the same time we will read and discuss texts that explore the experience of internal struggle, the tension between self and other, and the shift from outsider to insider perspectives. Because we are each shaped by distinct factors (e.g., gender, race, socioeconomic background, geographical origin, ethnicity, age, etc.), we are always in the midst of human difference. How we respond to that difference shapes our relation to others and to institutions.

Field Project Description

The field project in this course will evolve over the course of the semester. As you carry out a particular phase of fieldwork, you will write what becomes an eventual subdivision of a larger research paper. Writing and revising over time, you will produce a single document of considerable substance. Here are the units of the course that will correspond with your fieldwork, reading, and writing:

Unit One: Examining the Self

Unit Two: Entering the Field

Unit Three: Interviewing Informants

Unit Four: Coming to Conclusions

Unit #1: Examining the Self

During the early weeks of this semester, I have emphasized the significance of reading as a critical activity. Just recently, we have expanded our notion of critical reading to include the critical analysis of cultural life. We have shifted from the question "Why do writers make the specific textual choices they do and how, specifically, do these choices influence a text?" to "Why do members of particular subcultures make the specific choices they do (artifacts, rituals, language, and stories) and what, specifically, do these features of cultural life suggest about their perspective?" Understanding how texts and people function is an important critical process. When we overlook the features of what we read and experience, we are open to manipulation. To be a critical reader, writer, and human being, we must constantly interpret what we live.

The introductory subdivision of your longer field project will introduce your topic to the reader. The introduction articulates what subculture you have selected and explores the outsider, or etic, perspective you hold prior to fieldwork. In other words, the introduction identifies specifically how you have come to assume or know what you do about the subculture you have chosen. Your introduction should address the following issues central to any study of culture.

1. Introduction of the topic and guiding questions:

   We'll talk in class about strategies for introducing a paper or project. There exist various ways you might escort readers into your project. Here are some issues you might address:

   a. How you came to be interested in the subculture you've selected,

   b. What you hope to learn/accomplish by researching the subculture you've chosen,

   c. How you believe this information might be useful to you and others, and

   d. The guiding questions that will frame your study.

2. Exploration of your outsider perspective. Once you've introduced readers to your topic and your guiding questions, you're ready to explore how particular experiences in your life have shaped the perspective you hold at the start of your study. What experiences in your home and community life have shaped beliefs that may influence your perception of this subculture? How can you reflect on these experiences with description and analysis so that readers understand their effect on your perspective?

Unit #2: Entering the Field

Now that each of you has selected and introduced a field project, as well as secured approval with this group, you are prepared to begin the actual process of investigating the practices and perspectives of members of this subculture. You have several obligations during the next three weeks of observation:

1. Conduct at least two visits to the site where members of the subculture gather.

2. Use formal fieldnoting strategies as you describe and interpret artifacts, language, rituals, people, and place.

3. Avoid subjective language in *all* fieldnotes and written drafts.

4. Collect extensive initial fieldnotes so that you will have the data you need to compose your arrival narrative.

5. Put all fieldnotes, drafts, and fieldwork artifacts in your binder. They are a record of your research process that I will require at the end of the semester. I recommend that you collect fieldnotes in your composition book.

Collecting Fieldnotes During this stage of your project, you will be "stepping in" to the subculture you've elected to study. This stage of your research takes considerable powers of observation. In order to collect data in a systematic way, I ask that you collect what anthropologists call "initial fieldnotes." These are the actual notes you create as you observe members of the subculture. Because this is the data upon which your eventual subdivision will be crafted, capture as much information as possible.

a. *In the left-hand column of your fieldnotes:* Record descriptive details about artifacts, rituals, language, place, and person. Quote language directly rather than paraphrasing in your own words.

Describe Place
Begin recording from a focal point and continue recording details through the recesses of the space.
Sources of Description
- *Record:* map the site (note features of landscape, interior space)

Describe Person
Observe systematically (from head to toe, individual to individual).
Sources of Description
- *Record:* physical features of members
- *Record:* material possessions (clothing, accessories) that distinguish each member
- *Record:* members' movement and gestures

Describe Rituals
Note physical behaviors of individuals and group from beginning to end of observation.
Sources of Description
- *Record:* rituals of those most visibly in a position of power to those seemingly least powerful
- *Record:* common behaviors of group members
- *Record:* who initiates and sustains rituals

Describe Language
Note verbal behaviors of individuals and group from beginning to end of observation.
Sources of Dialogue
- *Record:* jokes, stories, and objects that members articulate
- *Record:* formal and informal language shared between members
- *Record:* shared phrases that members repeat or say together

b. *In the right-hand column of your fieldnotes* (after you've left the site): Reflect on what the descriptive data you've recorded may suggest, as well as what questions the data raise.

Sources of Interior Monologue
- *Reflect:* interpret what the arrangement of place might suggest about the status of the subculture, about the power differentials among members, about the significance of place to group identity.
- *Reflect:* interpret any common physical or material features for what they might suggest about identities and relationships.
- *Reflect:* interpret what the individual and collective rituals indicate about the subculture. Consider how rituals reflect differences arising from personality, gender, age, racial/ethnic difference.
- *Reflect:* interpret language for how it is used to assert power or to negotiate group identity. Who speaks? Who doesn't? What do distinctive features of language use reveal about the subculture? How do members convey meaning through stories, lore, or humor?
- *Reflect:* interpret any tensions you experienced as you observed members of the subculture. Think deeply about how your own experiences, beliefs, values, or language influenced your perception. Attempt to explain tensions you felt not by asserting the rightness of your history, but by contemplating the differences in experience between you and informants. Do this by identifying the particular tensions you experienced during observation. Then think about how these differences of perspective or practice may represent distinct cultural histories. This process is a way of understanding informants through their histories not just your own.

Writing the Arrival Narrative The arrival narrative recounts what you observed in the fullest and most vivid way. Your arrival narrative may reflect your single visits or be composed as a single visit incorporating all the details you gathered during the observational period. Keep in mind that your arrival narrative should also incorporate any moments of tension you experienced as an observer. As researcher–narrator, create an arrival narrative that allows readers to understand and follow your entrance into the subculture. You must convince your reader that you have entered the subculture with a critical eye. This subdivision sustains the "I" first person. A host of strategies will help you produce what anthropologists call "thick description":

1. Vivid description of person and place.
2. Dialogue to capture the language, tone, and demeanor of members.
3. Interior monologue to reveal your own thoughts, questions, and interpretation.

Unit #3: Interviewing Informants

Now that each of you has introduced a field project and created a narrative portrait of your arrival, you are prepared to begin the actual process of interviewing members of the subculture. At this point, you have monitored your assumptions regarding the subculture, and you've entered into that group to observe artifacts, rituals, and language for what they imply about informants' perspectives and practices. Given what you have observed, you are ready to enter into the next phase of research. *Interviewing* at least three informants in your subculture will be a way of testing certain questions that have entered your mind during the course of your study.

Creating Interview Questions The interviewing phase begins with question-making. Prior to actually speaking to informants, you must create the questions that will form the context of your interview. You will ask each of your three informants the same set of closed and open questions. This procedure will allow you to look across your data to determine how informants perceive their subculture similarly and differently. Begin by analyzing your guiding questions and fieldnotes. What questions did you isolate at the onset of this study? What subsequent questions arose during observation?

Your script of questions will contain two types, closed and open. *Closed questions* ask informants for specific details that you can later weave into an informant sketch. Closed questions should be relevant to the study you're conducting. Most importantly, they should not be intrusive. These questions provide data that is often useful as biographical information in your informant sketches. *Open questions* are the workhorse variety that provide you much data. They are questions that invite informants to speak in more expanded detail about their subculture. Put simply, open questions invite longer stretches of talk.

How to Interview Given the rich data you will receive from informants, it's important that you find a systematic and reliable way of collecting the data. Many ethical dimensions play into this stage.

Ethical Dimension #1: Research of this kind demands that you receive formal written consent prior to the actual interview. This consent procedure is required by law in most states. All informants must understand (a) that they have the right to anonymity, (b) that they have the right to review how their words appear in print, (c) that they have a right, at any time, to pull out of the project.

Ethical Dimension #2: In addition to receiving permission to cite informants, it's important you textualize, or write them up, accurately. How you collect verbal data is important. I recommend one of the following two approaches:

  a. *Use an audiocassette tape to record your interview.* This will allow you to return to the tape and transcribe the passages you wish to use in your informant sketch.
  b. *Correspond with your informants by email.* The obvious advantage here is time. Since your informants will provide you a text of their own words, you will not need to transcribe from audiotape. The disadvantage, which can be important, is that you are not in a position to observe the informant during the interview session, a time when you can more easily extend conversation.

Creating the Informant Sketch When you have transcribed the verbal data from audiotape that you wish to use and when you have fieldnotes from the interview beside you, you're ready to begin composing an informant sketch for each of the three people you have interviewed. The informant sketch provides readers a sense for each individual with whom you conversed. An effective sketch provides readers

  a. extended comment from the informant,
  b. descriptive details about the context of the interview, and
  c. reflective insights from the researcher.

The informant sketch is a portrait of a single person/perspective. The more the sketch allows readers to see, hear, and observe the interview—as if they were there—the more effective the sketch.

Unit #4: Coming to Conclusions

Now that each of you has introduced a field project, created an arrival narrative, and captured the perspective of your informants, you are prepared to conclude the field project. The conclusion is a subdivision in which you consider the entire process of fieldwork. How you conclude your field project depends upon the particularities of your study. Here are some suggestions:

  a. What key themes did you discover across your complete set of data? In light of your observations and across the data you collected through interviews, what seem to be key themes? We will talk about the process of "triangulation" in class.

b. Return to the etic (outsider) perspective that you identified prior to fieldwork. As a result of your observations and interviews, how has your perspective changed? How, in other words, has your own positionality as a researcher and human being been influenced by those who hold an emic (insider) perspective?

Remember that the conclusion is not about making generalizations. You can only identify common themes in terms of the particular group you investigated.

Appendix B: Performance Theory
and Body Theory Reading List

Performance Theory Readings: Summer Term 1993

Austin, J. L. 1975. *How to Do Things with Words*. Cambridge, MA: Harvard University Press.

Bateson, G. 1972. *Steps Toward an Ecology of Mind*. New York: Chandler Publishing.

Bauman, R. 1973. *Verbal Art as Performance*. New York: Ballentine Books.

———. 1986. *Story, Performance, and Event: Contextual Studies of Oral Narrative*. Cambridge Studies in Oral and Literature Culture Series, 10. Cambridge, MA: Harvard University Press.

———. 1989. "American Folklore Studies and Social Transformation: A Performance-Centered Perspective." *Text and Performance Quarterly* 9: 175–184.

———. 1992. "Performance." In *Folklore, Cultural Performances, and Popular Entertainments*, ed. R. Bauman. New York: Oxford University Press.

Bauman, R. and C. Briggs. 1990. "Poetics and Performance as Critical Perspectives on Language and Social Life." *Annual Review of Anthropology* 19: 59–88.

Bruner, E. 1984. *Text, Play, and Story: The Construction and Reconstruction of Self and Society*. Washington, D.C.: American Ethnological Society.

Caton, Stephen. 1985. "The Poetic Construction of Self." *Anthropological Quarterly* 5 (October): 141–151.

Enright, R. 1986. "To Dynamize the Audience: Interview with Augusto Boal." *Canadian Theatre Review* 47 (summer): 41–49.

Geertz, C. 1983. "'From the Native's Point of View': On the Nature of Anthropological Understanding." In *Local Knowledge*. New York: Basic Books.

Goffman, E. 1959. *The Presentation of Self in Everyday Life*. Garden City, NJ: Doubleday Anchor.

———. 1969. *Strategic Interaction*. Philadelphia: University of Pennsylvania Press.

———. 1983. "The Interaction Order." Presidential Address. *American Sociological Review* 48 (February): 1–17.

Harre, R. and P. F. Secord. 1972. *The Explanation of Social Behavior*. Totowa, NJ: Rowman and Littlefield.

Lord, A. B. 1960. *The Singer of Tales*. Cambridge, MA: Harvard University Press.

Myerhoff, B. 1978. *Number Our Days*. New York: Simon and Schuster.

Pelias, R. J. and J. Van Oosting. 1987. "A Paradigm for Performance Studies." *Quarterly Journal of Speech* 73 (May): 219–231.

Schechner, R. 1985. *Between Theater and Anthropology*. Philadelphia: University of Pennsylvania Press.

———. 1988. *Performance Theory*. New York: Routledge.

———. 1990. "Introduction." In *By Means of Performance,* eds. R. Schechner and W. Appel. Cambridge: Cambridge University Press.

———. 1990. "Magnitudes of Performance." In *By Means of Performance,* eds. R. Schechner and W. Appel. Cambridge: Cambridge University Press.

———. 1993. *The Future of Ritual: Writings on Culture and Performance*. London: Routledge.

———. 1993. "A New Paradigm for Theatre in the Academy." *TDR* 36 (winter): 7–10.

Scott, J. C. 1990. *Domination and the Arts of Resistance: Hidden Transcripts*. New Haven: Yale University Press.

Theory Readings: Spring Term 1994

Performance as Process and Event

Bauman, R. 1989. "American Folklore Studies and Social Transformation: A Performance-Centered Perspective." *Text and Performance Quarterly* 9: 175–184.

Bronner, S. J. 1988. "Art, Performance, and Praxis: The Rhetoric of Contemporary Folklore Studies." *Western Folklore* 47 (April): 75–102.

Conquergood, D. 1992. "Ethnography, Rhetoric, and Performance (Book Review)." *Quarterly Journal of Speech* 78: 80–123.

Turner, V. 1988. "Rokujo's Jealousy: Liminality and the Performative Genres." In *The Anthropology of Performance*. New York: PAJ Publications.

———. 1990. "The Anthropology of Performance." In *Victor Turner and the Construction of Cultural Criticism*, ed. K. M. Ashley. Bloomington: Indiana University Press.

Performance Events: Sites of Negotiated Ritual and Ethos

Duranti, A. 1986. "The Audience as Co-author." *Text* 6: 239–247.

Grimes, R. 1990. "Victor Turner's Definition, Theory, and Sense of Ritual." In *Victor Turner and the Construction of Cultural Criticism*, ed. K. M. Ashley. Bloomington: Indiana University Press.

Moore, S. F. and B. G. Myerhoff. 1977. "Secular Ritual: Forms and Meanings." In *Secular Ritual*, eds. S. F. Moore and B. G. Myerhoff. Assen/Amsterdam: Van Gorcum.

Myerhoff, B. "We Don't Wrap Herring in a Printed Page: Fusion, Fictions, and Continuity in Secular Ritual." In *Secular Ritual*. eds. S. F. Moore and B. G. Myerhoff. Assen/Amsterdam: Van Gorcum.

Ong, W. J. 1975. "The Writer's Audience Is Always a Fiction." *PMLA* 90: 9–21.

Reynolds, N. 1993. "*Ethos* as Location: New Sites for Understanding Discursive Authority." *Rhetoric Review* 11 (spring): 324–338.

Said, E. 1983. "Opponents, Audiences, Constituencies, and Communities." In *The Anti-Aesthetic: Essays on Postmodern Culture*, ed. Hal Foster. Seattle: Bay Press.

Turner, T. 1977. "Transformation, Hierarchy and Transcendence: A Reformulation of Van Gennep's Model of the Structure of Rites de Passage." In *Secular Ritual*, eds. S. F. Moore and B. G. Myerhoff. Assen/Amsterdam: Van Gorcum.

Turner, V. 1969. *The Ritual Process*. Ithaca, NY: Cornell University Press.

Transforming Space and Situation Through Performance

Baudrillard, J. 1983. "The Ecstasy of Communication." In *The Anti-Aesthetic: Essays on Postmodern Culture*, ed. Hal Foster. Seattle: Bay Press.

Bennett, B. 1992. "Performance and the Exposure of Hermeneutics." *Theatre Journal* 44: 431–447.

Kugelmass, J. 1991. "Wishes Come True: Designing the Greenwich Village Halloween Parade." *Journal of American Folklore* 104: 443–465.

Myerhoff, B. and S. Mongulle. 1986. "The Los Angeles Jews' 'Walk for Solidarity': Parade, Festival, Pilgrimage." In *Symbolizing America*, ed. H. Varenne. Lincoln, NE: Univeristy of Nebraska Press.

Schechner, R. 1993. *The Future of Ritual*. London: Routledge.

Gender and Performance

Bell, E. 1993. "Performance Studies as Women's Work: Historical Sights/Sites/Citations from the Margin." *Text and Performance Quarterly* 13: 350–374.

Buker, E. 1991. "Rhetoric in Postmodern Feminism: Put-Offs, Put-Ons, and Political Plays." In *The Interpretive Turn*, eds. D. R. Hiley, J. F. Bohman, and R. Schusterman. Ithaca: Cornell University Press.

Capo, K. E. and D. M. Hantzis. "(En)Gendered (and Endangered) Subjects: Writing, Reading, Performing and Theorizing Feminist Criticism." *Text and Performance Quarterly* 11: 249–266.

Foster-Dixon, G. 1993. "Troping the Body: Etiquette Texts and Performance." *Text and Performance Quarterly* 13: 79–96.

Owens, C. 1983. "The Discourse of Others: Feminists and Postmodernism." In *The Anti-Aesthetic: Essays on Postmodern Culture*, ed. H. Foster. Seattle: Bay Press.

Sptzack, C. 1993. "The Spectacle of Anorexia Nervosa." *Text and Performance Quarterly* 13: 1–20.

Oral and Literate Performance in Schools

Dyson, A. H. 1992. "The Case of the Singing Scientist: A Performance Perspective on the 'Stages' of School Literacy." *Written Communication* 9 (January): 3–47.

Farr, M. 1993. "Essayist Literacy and Other Verbal Performances." *Written Communication* 10 (January): 4–38.

Fine, M. 1987. "Silencing in Public Schools." *Language Arts* 64 (February): 157–174.

Gilmore, P. 1985. "Silence and Sulking: Emotional Displays in the Classroom." In *Perspectives on Silence*, eds. D. Tannen and M. Saville-Troike. Norwood, NJ: Ablex Publishing.

Grumet, M. R. 1990. "On Daffodils that Come before the Swallow Dares." In *Qualitative Inquiry in Education: The Continuing Debate*, eds. E. W. Eisner and A. Peshkin. New York: Teachers College Press.

Langellier, K. M. 1989. "Personal Narratives: Perspectives on Theory and Research." *Text and Performance Quarterly* 9 (October): 243–276.

McLaren, P. 1988. "The Liminal Servant and the Ritual Roots of Critical Pedagogy." *Language Arts* 65 (February): 164–179.

Pineau, E. L. 1994. "Teaching Is Performance: Reconceptualizing a Problematic Metaphor." *American Educational Research Journal* 31 (spring): 3–25.

Spellmeyer, K. 1993. "Knowledge and Appropriation: Community or Communitas?" In *Common Ground: Dialogue, Understanding, and the Teaching of Composition*. Englewood Cliffs, NJ: Prentice Hall.

Sunstein, B. S. 1994. "'Ce Que J'eprouve': Grainstacks, Writing, and Open Spaces." *Education and Culture* 11 (fall): 17–27.

Tompkins, J. 1990. "Pedagogy of the Distressed." *College English* 52 (October): 643–660.

Trachsel, M. 1994. "Literacy as Performance: An Exploration for Teachers of English." Unpublished manuscript.

Body Theory and Related Readings: Fall Semester 1994

Argyle, M. 1975. *Bodily Communication*. New York: International Universities Press, Inc.

Bachelard, G. 1969. *The Poetics of Space*. Trans. M. Joles. Boston: Beacon Press.

Behar, B. 1993. *Translated Woman: Crossing the Border with Esperanza's Story*. Boston: Beacon Press.

Bilmes, J. and A. Howard. 1980. "Pain as Cultural Drama." *Anthropology and Humanism Quarterly* 5: 10–13.

Briggs, J. L. 1970. *Never in Anger: Portrait of an Eskimo Family.* Cambridge, MA: Harvard University Press.

Butler, J. 1990. *Gender Trouble: Feminism and the Subversion of Identity.* New York: Routledge.

Dominguez, V. R. 1994. "A Taste for 'the Other': Intellectual Complicity in Racializing Practices." *Current Anthropology* 35:4: 333–348.

Fabian, J. 1990. *Power and Performance: Ethnographic Explorations through Proverbial Wisdom in Theater in Shaba, Zaire.* Madison: University of Wisconsin Press.

———. 1993. *Time and the Other: How Anthropology Makes Its Object.* New York: Columbia University Press.

Grosz, E. 1994. *Volatile Bodies: Toward a Corporeal Feminism.* Bloomington: Indiana University Press.

Jackson, M. 1989. *Paths toward a Clearing: Radical Empiricism and Ethnographic Inquiry.* Bloomington: Indiana University Press.

Johnson, M. 1987. *The Body in the Mind: The Bodily Basis of Meaning, Imagination, and Reason.* Chicago: University of Chicago Press.

Lavie, S. 1990. *The Poetics of Military Occupation.* Berkeley: University of California Press.

Lewis, M. and R. I. Simon. 1986. "A Discourse Not Intended for Her: Learning and Teaching within Patriarchy." *Harvard Education Review* 56: 457–492.

Lutz, C. and L. Abu-Lughod. *Language and the Politics of Emotion.* New York: Cambridge University Press.

Madison, D. S. 1993. "'That Was My Occupation': Oral Narrative, Performance, and Black Feminist Thought." *Text and Performance Quarterly* 13:3: 213–232.

McLaren, P. 1985. "The Ritual Dimensions of Resistance: Clowning and Symbolic Inversion." *Journal of Education* 167: 84–97.

———. 1993. *Schooling as a Ritual Performance: Towards a Political Economy of Educational Symbols and Gestures.* New York: Routledge.

Nash, J. 1979. *We Eat the Mines and the Mines Eat Us: Dependency and Exploitation in Bolivian Tin Mines.* New York: Columbia University Press.

Ness, S. A. 1992. *Body, Movement, and Culture: Kinesthetic and Visual Symbolism in a Philippine Community.* Philadelphia: University of Pennsylvania Press.

Polhemus, T. 1978. *The Body Reader: Social Aspects of the Human Body.* New York: Pantheon.

Scheff, T. J. 1977. "The Distancing of Emotion in Ritual." *Current Anthropology* 18: 483–504.

Scheper-Hughes, N. 1992. *Death without Weeping: The Violence of Everyday Life in Brazil.* Berkeley: University of California Press.

Sklar, D. 1994. "Can Bodylore Be Brought to Its Senses?" *Journal of American Folklore* 107: 9–22.

Smith, S. 1993. *Subjectivity, Identity, and the Body: Women's Autobiographical Practices in the Twentieth Century*. Bloomington: Indiana University Press.

Strine, M. S., B. W. Long, and M. F. Hopkins. "Research in Interpretation and Performance Studies: Trends, Issues, Priorities." In *Speech Communication: Essays to Commemorate the 75th Anniversary of The Speech Communication Association*, eds. G. M. Phillips and J. T. Wood. Carbondale: Southern Illinois University Press.

Tuan, Yi-Fu. 1977. *Space and Place: The Perspective of Experience*. Minneapolis: University of Minnesota Press.

Williams, P. 1991. *The Alchemy of Race and Rights: Diary of a Law Professor*. Cambridge, MA: Harvard University Press.

Young, K. 1994. "Whose Body? An Introduction to Bodylore." *Journal of American Folklore* 107: 3–8.

Bibliography

"A Brief Guide to the *Rutgers Magazine Censorship Controversy." Rutgers 1000*. 1999. http://members.aol.com/rualliance/censor.html.

Abu-Lughod, L. 1991. "Writing Against Culture." In *Recapturing Anthropology*, ed. R. G. Fox. Santa Fe, NM: School of American Research Press.

———. 1993. "Can There Be a Feminist Ethnography?" *Women and Performance* 5: 7–27.

American Institute for Research. 1989. *Studies of Intercollegiate Athletics*. Palo Alto, CA: Center for the Study of Athletics.

Applebee, A. 1974. *Tradition and Reform in the Teaching of English: A History*. Urbana, IL: National Council of Teachers of English.

Bachelard, G. 1969. *The Poetics of Space*. Transl. M. Jolas. Boston: Beacon Press.

Baktin, M. 1981. *Speech Genres and Other Late Essays*. Trans. V. W. McGee. Austin: University of Texas Press.

Bassinger, J. 1997. "Black and Low-Income Students Feel Impact of More Rigorous NCAA Eligibility Rules." *The Chronicle of Higher Education* 1 (9 Sept): A48.

Bauman, R. 1977. *Verbal Art as Performance*. Prospect Heights, IL: Waveland Press.

Bean, R. 1906. "Some Racial Peculiarities of the Negro Brain." *American Journal of Anatomy* 5: 353–432.

Becker, A. 1995. *Body, Self, and Society: The View from Fiji*. Philadelphia: University of Pennsylvania Press.

Behar, R. 1993. *Translated Woman: Crossing the Border with Esperanza's Story*. Boston: Beacon Press.

Benton, C. 1993. "Performance: Ethical Concerns and Moral Dilemmas." *Text and Performance Quarterly* 13: 97–111.

Beran, J. 1993. *From Six-on-Six to Full Court Press: A Century of Iowa Girls' Basketball*. Ames, IA: Iowa State University Press.

Berlin, J. 1988. "Rhetoric and Ideology in the Writing Class." *College English* 50:5 (September): 477–494.

Blais, M. 1995. *In These Girls, Hope is a Muscle*. New York: Warner Books.

Bodley, J. H. 1988. *Tribal Peoples and Development Issues: A Global Overview*. Mountain View, CA: Mayfield.

Bogdan, R. J. 2000. *Minding Minds*. Cambridge, MA: MIT Press.

Bollig, L. E. 1993. *Official 1994 NCAA Basketball*. Overland Park, KS: National Collegiate Athletic Association.

Bordo, S. 1993. *Unbearable Weight: Feminism, Western Culture, and the Body*. Berkeley: University of California Press.

Briggs, C. 1984. "Learning How to Ask: Native Metacommunicative Competence and the Incompetence of Fieldworkers." *Language in Society* 13: 1–28.

Briggs, J. L. 1970. *Never in Anger: Portrait of an Eskimo Family*. Cambridge, MA: Harvard University Press.

Brinton, D. 1890. *Races and Peoples*. New York: N.D.C. Hodges.

Bruner, J. 1978. *Human Growth and Development*. Oxford: Clarendon Press.

———. 1986. *Actual Minds, Actual Worlds*. Cambridge, MA: Harvard University Press.

Burger, J. 1990.*The Gaia Atlas of First Peoples: A Future for the Indigenous World*. London: Gaia Books.

Butler, J. 1993. *Bodies That Matter: On the Discursive Limits of "Sex."* New York: Routledge.

Buttimer, A. 1993. *Geography and the Human Spirit*. Baltimore, MD: Johns Hopkins University Press.

Carpsecken, P. 1993. "Afterword." In *Schooling as a Ritual Performance: Towards a Political Economy of Educational Symbols and Gestures*, P. McLaren 2nd ed. London: Routledge.

Casey, E. 1993. *Getting Back into Place: Toward a Renewed Understanding of the Place-World*. Bloomington: Indiana University Press.

———. 1996. "How to Get from Space to Place." In *Senses of Place*, eds. S. Feld and K. H. Basso. Santa Fe, NM: School of American Research Press.

Cazden, C. B. 1988. *Classroom Discourse: The Language of Teaching and Learning*. Portsmouth, NH: Heinemann.

Chapman, P. 1988. *Schools as Sorters: Lewis M. Terman, Applied Psychology, and the Intelligence Testing Movement: 1890–1930*. New York: New York University Press.

Cheville, J., et al. 1994. "Performance Theory: A Colloquium." Unpublished manuscript.

Chiseri-Strater, E. and B. S. Sunstein. 2000. *FieldWorking: Reading and Writing Research*. New York: Bedford/St. Martin's.

Clifford, J. 1983. "On Ethnographic Authority." *Representations* 2 (1): 118–146.

Cohen, D. 1976. "Loss as a Theme in Social Policy." *Harvard Educational Review* 46: 553–571.

Connerton, P. 1989. *How Societies Remember*. Cambridge: Cambridge University Press.

Cope, E. 1887. *The Origin of the Fittest*. New York: Macmillan.

Crapanzano, V. 1990. "On Dialogue." In *The Interpretation of Dialogue*, ed. T. Maranhao. Chicago: University of Chicago Press.

Crossley, N. 1996. *Intersubjectivity: The Fabric of Social Becoming*. London: Sage.

Crowley, S. 1998. *Composition in the University: Historical and Polemical Essays*. Pittsburgh: University of Pittsburgh.

Csordas, T. 1994. *Embodiment and Experience: The Existential Ground of Culture and Self*. Cambridge: Cambridge University Press.

Damasio, A. R. 1994. *Descartes' Error: Emotion, Reason, and the Human Brain*. New York: Avon Books.

———. 1999. *The Feeling of What Happens: Body and Emotion in the Making of Consciousness*. New York: Harcourt Brace and Company.

Degler, C. 1991. *In Search of Human Nature: The Decline and Revival of Darwinism in American Social Thought*. New York: Oxford University Press.

Dohrmann, G. 1999. "U Rules Four Players Ineligible to Play." *The Pioneer Press* 11 (March): 1A.

Dongoske, K., T. J. Ferguson, and M. Yeatts. 1994. "Ethics of Field Research for the Hopi Tribe." *Anthropology Newsletter* (January): 56–57.

Douglas, M. C. 1966. *Purity and Danger: An Analysis of the Concepts of Pollution and Taboo*. London: ARK Paperbacks.

DuBois, W. E. B. 1990. *The Souls of Black Folk*. New York: Vintage Books.

DuPlessis, R. B. 1985. *Writing beyond the Ending: Narrative Strategies of Twentieth-Century Women Writers*. Bloomington: Indiana University Press.

Dyson, A. H. 1992. "The Case of the Singing Scientist: A Performance Perspective on the 'Stages' of School Literacy." *Written Communication* 9: 3–47.

Emerson, R. M., R. I. Fretz, and L. L. Shaw. 1995. *Writing Ethnographic Fieldnotes*. Chicago: University of Chicago Press.

Engestrom, Y., R. Miettinen, R. Punamaki, and R-L. Punamaki. 1999. *Perspectives on Activity Theory*. Cambridge, UK: Cambridge University Press.

Entrikin, J. N. 1991. *The Betweenness of Place: Toward a Geography of Modernity*. Baltimore, MD: Johns Hopkins University Press.

Erickson, F. 1988. "An Anthropologist's Perspective." In *Perspectives on Literacy*, eds. E. R. Kintgen, B. M. Kroll, and M. Rose. Carbondale, IL: Southern Illinois University.

Eysenck, H. 1971. *IQ Argument: Race, Intelligence, and Education*. New York: Library Press.

Fabian, J. 1990. *Power and Performance: Ethnographic Explorations through Proverbial Wisdom and Theater in Shaba, Zaire*. Madison: University of Wisconsin.

———. 1993. *Time and the Other: How Anthropology Makes Its Object*. New York: Columbia University Press.

Fiske, J. 1993. *Power Plays, Power Works*. New York: Verso.

Foley, J. and T. Wirt. 1999. *Iowa Hawkeyes: 1999–2000 Basketball Media Guide*. Iowa City, IA: UI Printing Services.

Fordham, S. 1993. "Those Loud Black Girls": (Black) Women, Silence, and Gender 'Passing' in the Academy." *Anthropology and Education Quarterly* 24: 3–32.

Foucault, M. 1984. "Docile Bodies." In *The Foucault Reader*, ed. Paul Rabinow. New York: Pantheon Books.

Fox, R. G. 1991. *Recapturing Anthropology*, ed. R. G. Fox. Santa Fe: School of American Research Press.

Frey, D. 1994. *The Last Shot: City Streets, Basketball Dreams*. Boston: Houghton Mifflin Company.

Funk, G. D. 1991. *Major Violation: The Unbalanced Priorities in Athletics and Academics*. Champaign, IL: Leisure Press.

Gallop, J., ed. 1995. *Pedagogy: The Question of Impersonation*. Bloomington: Indiana University Press.

Galton, F. 1884. *Hereditary Genius*. New York: D. Appleton.

Gardner, H. 1983. *Frames of Mind: The Theory of Multiple Intelligences*. New York: Basic.

Giroux, H. A. 1993. *Border Crossings: Cultural Workers and the Politics of Education*. New York: Routledge.

Gissendanner, C. H. 1994. "African-American Women and Competitive Sport, 1920–1960." In *Women, Sport, and Culture*, eds. S. Birrell and C. L. Cole. Champaign, IL: Human Kinetics.

Goffman, E. 1959. *The Presentation of Self in Everyday Life*. Garden City, New York: Doubleday Anchor Books.

———. 1969. *Strategic Interaction*. Philadelphia: University of Pennsylvania Press.

Gould, S. 1981. *The Mismeasure of Man*. New York: W. W. Norton.

Grant, C. and M. C. Curtis. 1995. "Women's Athletics: Herstory." In *1995–1996 Big Ten Women's Basketball Guide*, ed. M. Masters. Park Ridge, IL: Big Ten Conference.

Grant, M. 1916. *The Passing of the Great Race: Or, the Racial Basis of European History*. New York: C. Scribner.

Grosz, E. 1994. *Volatile Bodies: Toward a Corporeal Feminism*. Bloomington: Indiana University Press.

Gupta, A. and J. Ferguson. 1992. "Beyond 'Culture': Space, Identity, and the Politics of Difference." *Cultural Anthropology* 7:1: 6–23.

Harris, J. 2000. "Meeting the New Boss, Same as the Old Boss: Class Consciousness in Composition." *CCC* 52:1 (September): 43–68.

Hawkins, B. 1995. "Examining the Experience of Black Student Athletes at Predominantly White NCAA Division I Institutions Using an Internal Colonial Model." Unpublished Ph.D. dissertation, University of Iowa.

Haworth, K. 1997. "Lawsuit Says NCAA's Eligibility Standards Are Racially Biased." *The Chronicle of Higher Education* (Jan. 17): A46.

Heath, S. B. 1984. *Ways with Words: Language, Life and Work in Communities and Classrooms*. Cambridge: Cambridge University Press.

Herrnstein, R. 1971. "IQ." *Atlantic Monthly* (September): 43–64.

————. 1994. *The Bell Curve: Intelligence and Class Structure in American Life*. New York: Free Press.

Hoberman, J. 1997. *Darwin's Athletes: How Sport Has Damaged Black America and Preserved the Myth of Race*. New York: Mariner.

hooks, b. 1993. *Sisters of the Yam: Black Women and Self-Recovery*. Boston: South End Press.

————. 1994. *Teaching to Transgress: Education as the Practice of Freedom*. New York: Routledge.

Horner, B. and M. Lu. 2000. *Representing the "Other": Basic Writers and the Teaching of Basic Writing*. Urbana, IL: NCTE.

Hudson, L. 1972. "The Context of the Debate." In *Race and Intelligence: The Fallacies behind the Race-IQ Controversy*, eds. K. Richardson and D. Spears. Baltimore: Penguin Books.

Hurston, Z. N. 1990. *Mules and Men*. New York: HarperCollins.

Jackson, P. and H. Delehanty. 1995. *Sacred Hoops: Spiritual Lessons of a Hardwood Warrior*. New York: Hyperion.

Jensen, A. 1969. "How Much Can We Boost IQ and Scholastic Achievement?" *Harvard Education Review* 39: 1–123.

Johnson, M. 1987. *The Body in the Mind: The Bodily Basis of Meaning, Imagination, and Reason*. Chicago: University of Chicago Press.

Kevles, D. J. 1984. "Annals of Eugenics: A Secular Faith—1." *The New Yorker* 60:8 (October): 52–125.

Kirschner, D. and J. A. Whitson. 1997. *Situated Cognition: Social, Semiotic, and Psychological Perspectives*. Mahwah, NJ: Lawrence Erlbaum Associates.

Koch, J. V. 1994. "A Troubled Cartel: The NCAA." *Law and Contemporary Problems* 38: 135–150.

Kolodny, A. 1998. *Failing the Future: A Dean Looks at Higher Education in the Twenty-first Century*. Durham, NC: Duke University Press.

Komesaroff, P. A., ed. 1995. *Troubled Bodies: Critical Perspectives on Postmodernism, Medical Ethics, and the Body*. Durham, NC: Duke University Press.

Kuhl, S. 1994. *The Nazi Connection: Eugenics, American Racism, and German National Socialism*. New York: Oxford University Press.

Kupfer, F. 1995. "Football's Awesome Mythological Status Is Bewildering." Editorial. *Ames Daily Tribune* (17 March): 9A.

Kupfer, J. 1995. "Sport—The Body Electric." In *Philosophic Inquiry in Sport*, eds. W. J. Morgan and K. V. Meier. Champaign, IL: Human Kinetics.

Labov, W. 1969. *The Logic of Non-Standard English*. Monograph Series on Language and Linguistics, 22. Washington, DC.: Georgetown University Press.

Ladson-Billings, G. 1992. *The Dreamkeepers: Successful Teachers of African-American Children*. San Francisco: Jossey-Bass.

Lakoff, G. 1989. *More than Cool Reason: A Field Guide to Poetic Metaphor*. Chicago: University of Chicago Press.

Lapchick, R. 1989. *Pass to Play: Student Athletes and Academics*. Washington, D.C.: National Education Association.

Larson, E. 1995. *Sex, Race, and Science: Eugenics in the Deep South*. Baltimore, MD: Johns Hopkins University Press.

Lave, J. 1997. "The Culture of Acquisition and the Practice of Understanding." In *Situated Cognition: Social, Semiotic, and Psychological Perspectives*, eds. D. Kirschner and J. A. Whitson. Mahwah, NJ: Lawrence Erlbaum Associates.

Lave, J. and E. Wenger. 1991. *Situated Learning: Legitimate Peripheral Participation*. Cambridge: Cambridge University Press.

Lavie, S. 1990. *The Poetics of Military Occupation*. Berkeley: University of California Press.

Lavin, D. E. and D. Hyllegard. 1996. *Changing the Odds: Open Admissions and the Life Chances of the Disadvantaged*. New Haven: Yale UP.

Lock, M. and N. Scheper-Hughes. 1987. "The Mindful Body." *Medical Anthropology Quarterly* 1: 6–41.

Lofland, J. 1984. "Erving Goffman's Sociological Legacies." *Urban Life* 13 (April): 7–34.

Lombroso, C. 1911. *Crime: Its Causes and Remedies*. Boston: Little, Brown.

Lunsford, A. 1991. "Collaboration, Control, and the Idea of a Writing Center." *The Writing Center Journal* 12:1 (fall): 3–10.

Mahala, D. and J. Swilky. 1996. "Telling Stories, Speaking Personally: Reconsidering the Place of Lived Experience in Composition." *Journal of Advanced Composition* 16:3: 363–388.

Marcus, G. E. 1994. "What Comes (Just) After 'Post'? In *Handbook of Qualitative Research*, eds. N. Denzin and Y. S. Lincoln. Thousand Oaks, CA: Sage.

Mauss, M. 1973. "The Techniques of the Body." Trans. B. Brewster. *Economy and Society* 2 (February): 70–88.

McCallum, J. 1995. "Out of Joint." *Sports Illustrated* 82 (February 13): 44–48.

McLaren, P. 1993. *Schooling as a Ritual Performance: Toward a Political Economy of Educational Symbols and Gestures*. New York: Routledge.

———. 1995. *Critical Pedagogy and Predatory Culture*. London: Routledge.

McPhee, J. 1999. *A Sense of Where You Are*. 2nd ed. New York: Noonday Press.

Merleau-Ponty, M. 1962. *Phenomenology of Perception*. Trans. C. Smith. London: Routledge.

Morris, D. 1991. *The Culture of Pain*. Berkeley: University of California Press.

Murphy, M. 2000. "New Faculty for a New University: Toward a Full-Time Teaching-Intensive Faculty Track in Composition." *CCC* 52:1 (September): 14–42.

Myerhoff, B. G. 1975. "Organization and Ecstasy: Deliberate and Accidental Communitas Among Huichol Indians and American Youth." In *Symbol and*

Politics in Communal Ideology, eds. S. F. Moore and B. G. Myerhoff. Ithaca: Cornell University Press.

———. 1978. *Number Our Days*. New York: Simon and Schuster.

Naismith, J. 1996. *Basketball: Its Origin and Development*. Lincoln: University of Nebraska Press.

National Alliance for College Athletic Reform. 2000. "The Drake Group." www.drake.edu/events/collegesports/meeting2results.html.

Nelson, M. B. 1994. *The Stronger Women Get, the More Men Love Football: Sexism and the American Culture of Sports*. New York: Harcourt, Brace and Company.

O'Donovan-Anderson, M. 1996. *The Incorporated Self: Interdisciplinary Perspectives on Embodiment*. Lanham, MD: Rowman and Littlefield.

Okely, J. 1992. "Anthropology and Autobiography: Participatory Experience and Embodied Knowledge." In *Anthropology and Autobiography*, eds. J. Okely and H. Callaway. London: Routledge.

Olson, A. 1991. *Body Stories: A Guide to Experiential Anatomy*. New York: Station Hill Press.

Palmer, P. 1997. *The Courage to Teach: Exploring the Inner Landscape of a Teacher's Life*. San Francisco: Jossey-Bass.

Pineau, E. 1994. "Teaching As Performance: Reconceptualizing a Problematic Metaphor." *American Educational Research Journal* 31: 3–25.

Pruden, V. 1987. *A Conceptual Approach to Basketball*. Champaign, IL: Leisure Press.

Qualley, D. 1997. *Turns of Thought: Teaching Composition as Reflexive Inquiry*. Portsmouth, NH: Boynton/Cook.

Reynolds, N. 1993. "*Ethos* as Location: New Sites for Understanding Discursive Authority." *Rhetoric Review* 11 (spring): 325–338.

Richardson, L. 1994. "Writing: A Method of Inquiry." In *Handbook of Qualitative Research*, eds. N. Denzin and Y. S. Lincoln. Thousand Oaks, CA: Sage.

Rogoff, B. 1995. "Observing Sociocultural Activity on Three Planes: Participatory Appropriation, Guided Participation, and Apprenticeship." In *Sociocultural Studies of Mind*, eds. J. V. Wertsch, P. Del Rio, and A. Alvarez. Cambridge: Cambridge University Press.

Root-Bernstein, R. and M. Root-Bernstein. 2000. "Learning to Think with Emotion." *The Chronicle of Higher Education* (January 14): A64.

Rothfield, P. 1995. "Bodies and Subjects: Medical Ethics and Feminism." In *Troubled Bodies: Critical Perspectives on Postmodernism, Medical Ethics, and the Body*, ed. P. A. Komesaroff. Durham, NC: Duke University Press.

Schechner, R. 1982. "Collective Reflexivity: Restoration of Behavior." In *A Crack in the Mirror: Reflexive Perspectives in Anthropology*, eds. B. G. Myerhoff and J. Ruby. Philadelphia: University of Pennsylvania Press.

———. 1985. *Between Theater and Anthropology*. Philadelphia: University of Pennsylvania.

————. 1988. *Performance Theory*. New York: Routledge.

————. 1993. *The Future of Ritual: Writings on Culture and Performance*. London: Routledge.

Scheper-Hughes, N. 1993. *Death without Weeping: The Violence of Everyday Life in Brazil*. Berkeley: University of California Press.

Schneekloth, L. H. and R. G. Shibley. 1995. *Placemaking: The Art and Practice of Building Communities*. New York: John Wiley & Sons.

Scribner, S. 1990. "A Sociocultural Approach to the Study of Mind." In *Theories of the Evolution of Knowing*, eds. G. Greenberg and E. Tobach. Hillsdale, NJ: Lawrence Erlbaum Associates.

Scribner, S. and M. Cole. 1981. *The Psychology of Literacy*. Cambridge: Harvard University Press.

Shotter, J. 1989. "Social Accountability and the Social Construction of 'You.'" In *Texts of Identity*, eds. J. Shotter and K. J. Gergen. London: Sage.

Siegle, R. 1986. *The Politics of Reflexivity: Narrative and the Constitutive Poetics of Culture*. Baltimore, MD: Johns Hopkins.

Smith, C. 1995. "A Coaching Legend Comes Home." *New York Times* (December 10): Y25.

Smith, S. 1993. *Subjectivity, Identity, and the Body: Women's Autobiographical Practices in the Twentieth Century*. Bloomington: Indiana University Press.

Sperber, M. 2000. *Beer and Circus: How Big-Time College Sports Is Crippling Undergraduate Education*. New York: Henry Holt.

Stocking, G. W., Jr. 1992. *The Ethnographer's Magic and Other Essays in the History of Anthropology*. Madison: University of Wisconsin Press.

Suggs, W. 1999a. "Fight Over NCAA Standards Reflects Long-Standing Dilemma." *The Chronicle of Higher Education* (April 9): A48.

————. 1999b. "Judge Refuses to Stay Ruling Barring NCAA's Use of Test Scores in Sports Eligibility." *The Chronicle of Higher Education* (March 26): A56.

————. 1999c. "Scandals Force Colleges to Reassesses Roles of Academic Advisors for Athletes." *The Chronicle of Higher Education* (December 3): A51.

Telander, R. 1995. *Heaven Is a Playground*. Lincoln: University of Nebraska Press.

Tuan, Y-F. 1977. *Space and Place: The Perspective of Experience*. Minneapolis, MN: University of Minnesota.

Turner, B. S. 1984. *The Body and Society: Exploratives in Social Theory*. New York: B. Blackwell.

————. 1992. *Regulating Bodies: Essays in Medical Sociology*. New York: Routledge.

Turner, T. 1994. "Bodies and Anti-Bodies: Flesh and Fetish in Contemporary Social Theory." In *Embodiment and Experience: The Existential Ground of Culture and Self*, ed. T. J. Csordas. Cambridge: Cambridge University Press.

Turner, V. 1969. *The Ritual Process: Structure and Anti-Structure*. Chicago: Aldine.

————. 1974. *Dramas, Fields, and Metaphors: Symbolic Action in Human Society*. Ithaca: Cornell University.

Twigg, R. 1994. "The Problem of 'Serious' Fiction: Modernization and the Textual Politics of Nineteenth-Century Literary Realism and Ethnography." *Text and Performance Quarterly* 14: 1–20.

van Gennep, A. 1960. *The Rites of Passage*. Chicago: University of Chicago Press.

Volosinov, V. N. 1986. *Marxism and the Philosophy of Language*. Trans. L. Matejka and I. R. Tutinik. Cambridge, MA: Harvard University Press.

Vygotsky, L. 1986. *Thought and Language*. Trans. A. Kozulin. Cambridge, MA: MIT Press.

Walkerdine, V. 1997. "Redefining the Subject in Situated Cognition Theory." In *Situated Cognition: Social, Semiotic, and Psychological Perspectives*, eds. D. Kirshner and J. A. Whitson. Mahwah, NJ: Lawrence Erlbaum Associates.

———. 1998. *Counting Girls Out*. London: Falmer Press.

Wenger, E. 1998. *Communities of Practice: Learning, Meaning, and Identity*. Cambridge: Cambridge University Press.

Wertsch, J. 1995. "The Need for Action in Sociocultural Research." In *Sociocultural Studies of Mind*, eds. J. Wertsch, P. Del Rio, and A. Alvarez. Cambridge: Cambridge University Press.

Wertsch, J., P. Del Rio, and A. Alvarez. 1995. *Sociocultural Studies of Mind*. Cambridge: Cambridge University Press.

Whitson, D. 1994. "Embodiment of Gender: Discipline, Domination, and Empowerment." In *Women, Sport, and Culture*, eds. S. Birrell and C. L. Cole. Champaign, IL: Human Kinetics.

Whitson, J. 1997. "Cognition as a Semiotic Process: From Situated Mediation to Critical Reflective Transcendence." In *Situated Cognition: Social, Semiotic, and Psychological Perspectives*, eds. D. Kirschner and J. A. Whitson. Mahwah, NJ: Lawrence Erlbaum Associates.

Wiener, H. 1998. "The Attack on Basic Writing—And After. *Journal of Basic Writing* 17:1 (spring): 96–103.

Wolf, M. 1992. *A Thrice-Told Tale: Feminism, Postmodernism, and Ethnographic Responsibility*. Stanford, CA: Stanford University Press.

Yamamoto, A. Y. 1979. *Culture Spaces in Everyday Life*. Publications in Anthropology 11. Lawrence, KS: University of Kansas Press.

Young, I. M. 1990. *Throwing Like a Girl and Other Essays in Feminist Philosophy and Social Theory*. Bloomington: Indiana University Press.

Young, K. 1994. "Whose Body? An Introduction to Bodylore." *Journal of American Folklore* 107: 3–8.

Index

164